# HAUNTED
# COTSWOLDS

## DIZ WHITE

117

The
History
Press

First published 2010

The History Press
The Mill, Brimscombe Port
Stroud, Gloucestershire, GL5 2QG
www.thehistorypress.co.uk

ISBN 978 0 7524 5426 9

Typesetting and origination by The History Press
Printed in Great Britain
Manufacturing managed by Jellyfish Print Solutions Ltd

# CONTENTS

# ABOUT THE AUTHOR

British-born Diz White, together with her husband Randall Montgomery whose photographs illustrate this book, divides her time between a career in Hollywood, USA, as an actress and screenplay writer, and her cottage in Gloucestershire, which she uses as a base for writing books about her beloved Cotswolds. In addition, she runs a DVD and mobile phone entertainment production company and can be reached through her website: www.dizwhite.com

Other books by Diz White:

*The Comedy Group Book* (Smith & Kraus).
*Haunted Cheltenham* (The History Press), to be published August 2010.
*Cheltenham: History You Can See* (The History Press), to be published 2011.

Diz is currently putting the finishing touches on her comedic memoir about the Cotswolds, *Life is Just a Bowl of Cherries: Fun Adventures Buying an English Country Cottage.*

# ACKNOWLEDGEMENTS

This book is dedicated to my husband Randall Montgomery, a professional photographer, who took all the photos for this book. I wish to thank him for these images, for his invaluable editing and computer expertise, and most of all for his incredible patience and hard work as he lovingly helped me put this book together. I also dedicate this book to my mother, the poet Josephine Ashley, and to my dear family.

I also wish to thank Monica B. Morris, author of *Goodnight Children, Everywhere: Voices of Evacuees* (The History Press) for her help, encouragement and superb editing skills.

This book would not have been possible without the vision of my commissioning editor, Nicola Guy. I wish to convey my thanks to her and her excellent team at The History Press.

Another thank you is gratefully given to all the helpful inhabitants of the Cotswolds, surely the most beautiful place on Earth, who told me their spooky stories and shared their ghostly haunts.

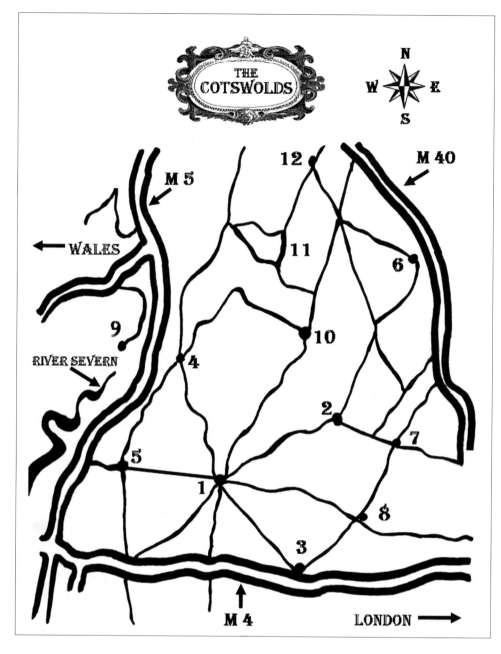

1. Cirencester
2. Burford
3. Swindon
4. Cheltenham
5. Stroud
6. Banbury
7. Oxford
8. Lechlade
9. Gloucester
10. Stow-on-the-Wold
11. Chipping Norton
12. Stratford-upon-Avon

# INTRODUCTION

This book guarantees a spine-chilling ride through the entire haunted Cotswolds region, with its surplus of spooks, spectres, glowing orbs, disembodied voices, phantoms, wraiths, banshees, shades, hobgoblins, ghouls, ghosts and the undead. All these entities will do their best to turn even the hardiest reader into a staring-eyed, gibbering, trembling blob who is assured terrifying dreams at night.

The unusual amount of ghostly activity noted in this region is most likely due to the perfect combination of the many gory battles fought throughout its history in the struggle for power and the fact that the Cotswolds is an ideal setting for otherworldly visitations.

The history of this area provides enough murder, mayhem, bloodshed, intrigue and treachery to prompt the spooky set to take up residence here, particularly after finding a comfortable home in many of the Cotswolds' centuries-old underground chambers, walled-off rooms, unexplored attics, lonely stagecoach routes, priest holes, ruined creepy castles and secret cellars. It is no wonder, therefore, that these spooks frequently run rampant, scaring the wits out of any poor soul they encounter.

The ghosts and other spectres that haunt this area are a creepy lot. There are headless kings, mad monks trailing blood, ghostly coaches and four, crying Cavaliers, an incubus and succubus, dematerializing dogs, invisible clanking chains, forlornly sobbing wraiths and preternatural poltergeists. All these entities seem to take delight in tormenting the inhabitants and visitors of this region; ghost hunters, however, are in for a lot of fun.

The grisly goings-on that unfolded in the Cotswolds, particularly after the Norman Conquest, must surely have been a catalyst for the large population of spectres who haunt the region to this day. Blood and gore were in good supply here, especially during the ruthless Roman occupation of Britain. At this time a large segment of the British population were forced into slavery and subjected to unspeakable torture. Back home in Italy, the typical Roman citizen's idea of a fun day out usually involved taking a picnic to the Coliseum in Rome and watching wild lions tear the heads off a bunch of Christians, so we can only imagine what these Romans did to the citizens of the lands they conquered. Despite their brutality, the Romans lived in an organised and sophisticated way, but when their empire unravelled England sank back into its previous barbarism.

For the next few centuries wild, marauding tribes roamed the land with many bloody battles being fought between the Mercian and Saxon kings. Next up was the Norman Conquest in 1066, with its virtual annihilation of the Saxon people. Following this even more blood was shed over the next several centuries as various monarchs struggled for power. it is not for nothing that the site of the Battle of Tewkesbury in 1471 became known as 'Bloody Meadow'.

Next, during Tudor times, the Dissolution of the Monasteries by Henry VIII led to the wholesale massacre of religious dissidents and, in addition, many priests of the Roman Catholic Church. Added to this were the fought-to-the-death battles between the Royalist and Parliamentarian forces in the English Civil War. The rich history of this area feels as if it unfolded just yesterday, perhaps because this parade of villains and victims lives on through their ghosts, many of which are described in this book.

The shades of plotting kings, wronged servants, treacherous Roundheads, intriguing earls, Gunpowder Plot conspirators, romantic highway robbers, hanging judges, lords of the manor, harried housekeepers and unpleasant pagans, among others, provided characters for these stories and all that was needed was the perfect setting. For this, the Cotswolds region fits the bill admirably.

This area extends south-west to north-east through six counties: Gloucestershire, Oxfordshire, Warwickshire, Somerset, Worcestershire and Wiltshire. Its exact boundaries are sometimes in dispute, but it lies approximately east of Wales with its southern edge ending a little below Bath. It extends north as far as Stratford-upon-Avon and its eastern boundary stretches from Swindon up to Banbury.

It is thought that the Cotswolds acquired its name from the sheep's enclosures or 'cots', combined with the description of the hills which were known during those times as 'wolds'. The thin soil here was not deemed suitable for arable farming but was ideal for raising sheep. These halcyon hills, so idyllic in the summer sunshine, can turn misty and mysterious at night. The long barrow burial mounds that are a feature of this region make eerie shadows in the light of the full moon. It seems that sometimes the long-dead souls inside them slip out of their resting place and roam the hills, causing consternation wherever they go.

Other mysterious forces are felt by many people who visit the Rollright Stones near Chipping Norton. These are a circle of ancient megaliths, somewhat similar in appearance to Stonehenge. There is a definite aura of spookiness around them and many hauntings must have originated from their Bronze Age beginnings. The Rollright Stones are situated on ancient ley lines. These lines, the study of which sceptics dub a pseudoscience, have been shown to align these megaliths with ancient sites of importance. It is well documented that ancient societies found it useful to establish tracks between important sites, and these would be marked in straight lines, some measuring hundreds of miles. The Rollright Stones site also seems to have been used over the centuries by a number of different religious sects and if the horrific tales of human sacrifice are true, they must surely have caused more than a little spiritual disturbance.

After the Norman Conquest in 1066, the Cotswolds prospered in a small way with sheep rearing and the trading of wool produced by the flocks that grazed its rolling hills. Several of the large market towns founded at this time were built around elaborate, perpendicular churches which became the salient feature of many of them.

The local stone is for the most part oolitic limestone and is used as the construction material for the cottages, manor houses, churches and drystone walls that give this area such a distinctive appearance. This stone varies in colour from pale ivory to a rich yellow-cream and when the sun sets it turns an attractive honey-tinted hue.

The skills learned from the Norman conquerors, who were expert masons, helped give the Cotswolds the unique appearance that it has to this day. Fine examples of stone cottages, parish churches, manor houses and barns are in abundant supply.

Wool production started even before the Roman occupation, literally as a cottage industry, and increased in importance over the next few hundred years. By the fifteenth century the entire area was heavily dependent upon it. The streams and rivers from the

*A spooky Cotswold gargoyle.*

steep hills of the western part of the Cotswolds provided the energy to power the mills. Money poured into the 'wool' churches, making them even grander, while large manor houses were also built to reflect the great prosperity of the time.

However, from 1700 until the mid-1800s, the Cotswolds' dominance in the wool trade dissipated as other wool producers competed against its output and won. This meant that there were no longer any funds for new building. It was this era of poverty that led to the Cotswolds of today having a 'frozen in time' appearance. It also saved it from the ugliness of Victorian remodelling which has blighted so many other areas of Great Britain. Thankfully the Cotswolds seems to have avoided the fate of this style of architecture, much of which appears to have won competitions for the 'Ugliest Building in Great Britain'. It is ironic that this lack of money contributed to the architectural unity that we see in the area today and which is now so highly valued. Nowadays, very little new building is allowed in the Cotswold area and what little there is has to blend in with the existing architectural styles. There are strict conservation rules in place and gaining new building permits can be very difficult. This all works to the Cotswold ghost population's advantage as these otherworldly visitors seem to prefer their original location to be undisturbed.

The spectres who have taken up residence, it seems, feel very much at home in the centuries-old Cotswolds buildings and churches where even the decorative elements lend themselves to a ghoulish atmosphere with their grotesque gargoyles, griffins, green men, misericords and macabre church effigies.

Surely, on a dark and misty night, a ghost would feel quite inclined to emanate from a good example of these ghastly church effigies, located in the twelfth-century St Mary's Church of the Virgin near the small village of Swinbrook in Oxfordshire. Here, wall tombs contain six life-sized marble likenesses of the male line of the Fettiplace family

*A church misericord.*

who lived close by for over four centuries. From the seventeenth century, this important landowning family commissioned these marble effigies for the church and they are to be found in the sanctuary and the choir. These very spooky marble figures are stacked one on top of another on stone shelves, almost as if they were reclining in bunk beds. Their gilded figures lean awkwardly on one elbow and are portrayed fully dressed, even wearing swords, gauntlets and lace jabots and sporting, in some cases, shoulder-length curly hair.

It is not hard to imagine an apparition rising out of these scary stone men in the middle of the night, carrying their disembodied souls with them as they restlessly roam the countryside. Church effigies such as these appear in a number of other Cotswold churches, including those at Chipping Norton and Burford.

Gargoyles also seem to attract ghosts as they are often exhibited with carved faces showing horrific expressions. The word 'gargoyle' is thought to be a translation of the French word *gargouille*, which means 'to gargle'. Often decorating the exterior of churches, gargoyles were originally used as rain spouts. Medieval stonemasons seemed to compete with each other in an effort to carve ever more grotesque visages. These gargoyles began to disappear after the innovation of downspouts in the eighteenth century. Other examples of church decorations include screaming monsters, serpents, devils, centaurs, daemons, cretins and fire-breathing dragons.

Another inspiration for ghosts is the grinning carvings of Green Men which adorn many churches and secular buildings in this area. These Green Men were first used as decorations during medieval times and their insanely grimacing and often menacing expressions are modelled on human likenesses which are then surrounded by carved foliage. During the pre-Christian era, these Green Men were used in pagan rituals, usually to signify the season of spring. Some of them are depicted as skeletons and appear to be haunting the churches they decorate.

Yet another scary architectural decoration seen in Cotswold churches and public buildings are griffins or, as they are sometimes known in Middle English, gryphons or griffons. These strange creatures are depicted as having lion's bodies and eagle's heads. This combination is meant to symbolise that griffins are both human and divine, and combine both great strength and intelligence. Their preternatural appearance, however, with their sharp eagle's claws and massive beaks, certainly contribute to a ghostly atmosphere when viewed in a dimly-lit ancient church.

The ghost stories in this book have all been well researched and documented by dozens of witnesses. Some manifestations have even been captured on film. Many sceptics scoff and dismiss ghost stories as 'a lot of old malarkey', but research into these sightings has shown that, on many occasions, witnesses have reported the same haunting independently of one another. Sometimes these reports have been hundreds of years apart and the witnesses were found to have had no previous knowledge of other, earlier sightings. In most cases these witnesses gave a description of a particular haunting that was amazingly similar, in every detail in fact, to previous reports.

According to J.A. Brooks in his book *The Ghosts and Witches of the Cotswolds*, in past times ghosts have been sufficiently disturbing for a recipe to be concocted by a Cotswold vicar in the seventeenth century for ridding a house of these spectres:

Lay a half pound of Brimstone [another word for sulphur in those times] in an iron dish, supported by a pair of tongs over a bucket of water; the fireplace and all openings to be closed, a shovelful of burning coal put on the brimstone, the door quickly shut and the room kept closed for six hours. This is one of the best ways of laying a ghost.

Perhaps some kind of fourth dimension exists in which shades reside and somehow they have the ability to repeatedly slip through a tear in the time/space continuum to make contact with mortals again. However it works, there is too much evidence of their existence for ghost hauntings to be discounted as a joke. The sceptics are challenged to be brave enough to read this book and remain unconvinced.

Those of you who already believe that visitations from the other side are a fact of life and know that ghosts walk among us can look forward to meeting a very interesting collection of creepy Cotswold spooks.

Because the Cotswolds is an area of outstanding natural beauty (it was designated as such in 1991), readers will also enjoy a virtual tour of the region as a pleasant addition to the chills and spills of the ghost stories themselves. In these pages there are anecdotes from Uley, Painswick, Wotton-Under-Edge, Minchinhampton, Gloucester, Burford, Banbury, Warwick, Faringdon and many other beautiful villages and towns.

The Cotswolds region is a well-known and loved tourist destination visited by holiday-makers from all over the world. Its chocolate-box-top, picture-perfect villages like Bibury, Upper and Lower Slaughter, Broadway and Bourton-on-the-Water, among others, are well worth a visit, but the wilder, less well-travelled spots in this area are of even more interest to those who delve into the paranormal. A visit to the windswept banks of the River Windrush, the remote trails of the Cotswold Way or the misty waters of the upper reaches of the Thames will enrich the reader's imagination and set the scene for the spooky tales that are told in these pages.

This book also includes a guided ghost tour of Chipping Norton and its surroundings. This haunted hotspot seems to be a particularly strong focus of spirit activity, so much so that an entire chapter has been devoted to describing the various apparitions that inhabit it. It would be good fun to pack a picnic lunch and charge off to 'Chippy', as this town is affectionately known by all who live there, and follow the haunted route laid out in this chapter. There is a map and directions to the locations of ghost sightings in Chipping Norton, but no guarantee that the thrill-seeking ghost hunter will come back unchanged by this experience. Even the most diehard sceptics have returned from this tour with a zombie-like expression, able only to make a request for a strong drink before stuttering out amazingly creepy experiences of things that go bump in the night. Good luck with this chapter and all the other stories written here, readers, and don't let the ghosts get you!

Princess Michael of Kent, who was born Baroness Marie-Christine von Beibnitz of Bohemia, was quoted as saying, 'I have no doubt that many old houses have some kind of spirit presence or ghost and, if Nether Lypiatt Manor has such, he, she or it must be benign and well disposed. We as a family have all been extremely happy living here'.

However, when interviewed, many inhabitants of the nearby villages did not agree with Princess Michael's portrayal of the friendly nature of the spirits that haunt the manor and told tales of two ghosts that have repeatedly returned over the centuries. These ghosts first appeared following the tenure of the manor's original owner, the aforementioned Judge John Coxe, or 'the Hanging Judge' as he was known.

This judge's son took his own life in Nether Lypiatt Manor and it is his ghost that is rumoured to have appeared in many of its rooms. Soul-shattering wails from this agonised apparition have scared almost every owner of the manor over the years.

In 1704, Judge Coxe presided over the case of a local blacksmith who had been convicted of murder. The judge initially sentenced him to hang but later, playing a cruel game, pledged to let the blacksmith go free if he could make a flawless set of wrought iron gates. The blacksmith worked almost without pause for fourteen days before delivering the finished artefacts. When the evil Judge Coxe examined them he found the smallest imperfection and did not allow the blacksmith a reprieve. This poor man was hanged on 25 January 1705.

On the anniversary of this date every year these same wrought iron gates, which adorn the entrance to the manor, are said to fly open at midnight to the accompaniment of eerie voices emanating from the trees surrounding the grounds. These sounds quickly climb to a screeching crescendo, at which point the ghost of the hanged blacksmith, riding a great white horse with hooves flying, thunders through the gates. Once outside, the apparition of the blacksmith's horse rears up on its hindquarters and, with great clouds of steam billowing from its nostrils, whinnies and snorts in the frosty night air. At the same time, the blacksmith's ghastly moans echo through Nether Lypiatt Manor and the surrounding grounds, sending chills through all who hear them.

# The Creepy Collector

## MORETON-IN-MARSH, GLOUCESTERSHIRE

Snowshill Manor was owned by Winchcombe Abbey from AD 821 until the Dissolution of the Monasteries in 1539. Its ownership then passed to the Crown and it was given to Catherine Parr, the wife of King Henry VIII. It is set in a remote part of the Cotswolds overlooking the Vale of Evesham and is surrounded by a series of terraced garden rooms.

The section of the manor now left standing was built in 1500 but, by 1919, after acquiring many owners, it was abandoned and left almost derelict. It was then bought by the eccentric architect and craftsman Charles Paget Wade from Suffolk, who was independently wealthy and able to indulge his mania for collecting. Charles Wade restored Snowshill and, from 1900 until the beginning of the 1950s, amassed the most extraordinary collection of everyday objects, eventually numbering over 22,000 items.

*Snowshill Manor, where a past owner is one of the undead.*

*Snowshill Manor from the garden.*

He used Snowshill Manor to house his collection, which included clocks, bicycles and children's toys. He augmented these items with more arcane ones such as collections of cow bells, butter stamps, automatons and twenty-six suits of samurai armour.

Wade also dabbled in alchemy, magic and, some say, the dark arts. He collected a number of artefacts that were connected with this interest and it is well documented that he would delight in deliberately scaring visitors to his mansion, including some members of the Bloomsbury Group, such as Virginia Woolf. As these visitors were viewing his collections he would slip unseen into the room that they were occupying and suddenly appear before them as if by magic. He became so adept at scaring his visitors that numbers of them were known to have fainted.

Charles Wade bought Snowshill Manor chiefly because it had no electricity. He felt that his collection would be enhanced by the spooky shadows cast by the oil lamps and candles that were used for illumination. Wade did not live in Snowshill itself but in the old priest's house in the courtyard, making the manor deserted by night; an ideal setting for the ghosts who were already present and for new ones who took up residence.

A dark hooded figure, widely believed to be a monk, has been reported haunting the manor on numerous occasions. He has been seen in the daytime, where it has been noted that he disturbs farm animals for several hundred yards around. His monk's habit swirls around him as he walks slowly around the mansion and seems to become illuminated from within. He has been known to kneel and appear to be praying before moving on, sometimes passing through walls, and at other times reclining on the stone floor.

Charles Wade donated Snowshill Manor to the National Trust, who took possession of it in 1951. After Wade's death, some of the manor staff ascertained that mysterious noises heard from behind closed doors were made by the ghost of the former owner.

Loud clanking and grating noises and sounds of grinding machinery echo through the deserted rooms of Snowshill Manor as, it seems, Charles Wade haunts his former home. He is apparently unable to leave behind his fantastic collection which he gathered obsessively for over fifty years.

# Miss Lobb's Lament

## KELMSCOTT, GLOUCESTERSHIRE

The famous Victorian designer and craftsman William Morris leased Kelmscott Manor jointly with the Pre-Raphaelite painter Dante Gabriel Rossetti in 1871 and made it his summer home. It is situated a couple of hundred yards or so from the River Thames on a quiet lane in the ancient village of Kelmscott.

Kelmscott Manor is primarily Tudor and was built in 1570. However, another wing was added in 1670. This house was chosen by Morris because it had remained largely unchanged by the original owners, a farming family called the Turners, for several hundred years. This three-storey, gabled, farmhouse-style building is made of traditional Cotswold limestone, while the added wing from around 100 years later shows the influence of the Renaissance with its classical pediments above the windows and fine wood panelling inside its rooms.

*A ghost haunts the attic of Kelmscott Manor.*

The manor has several attic rooms situated between the great timbers that support the roof where in earlier times, the tillers and herdsmen slept. These great timbers are exposed and provide a spooky setting for the ghost that is said to inhabit the upper rooms and roof of the manor. Morris's bedroom would make any ghost feel welcome because its seventeenth-century tapestry hangings show gruesome scenes of Samson having his eyes gouged out.

The manor is now owned by the Society of Antiquaries, who restored it and currently maintain it. It is open to the public on certain days in the summer months.

This beautiful old house, in its tranquil setting of semi-formal gardens surrounded by a halcyon meadow, hardly seems the setting for visitations from the other side. But according to some of the local villagers and volunteers who lead the tours of the manor, this is indeed the case.

After William Morris died, his daughter May took great care to guard his legacy and kept the manor exactly as her father had left it. The many textiles and wallpapers he produced, featuring patterns inspired by the surrounding flora and fauna, are still sold today and are displayed around the manor along with original furniture, metalwork, ceramics and other artefacts from Morris's craftwork.

For many years May Morris enjoyed the friendship of Miss Lobb, a close companion. Apparently Miss Lobb could be somewhat intimidating and even managed to scare

William Morris's friend, the formidable George Bernard Shaw, on one occasion when he came to tea.

When May died Miss Lobb was inconsolable and before very long, it is said, took a bottle of brandy and a shotgun to bed with her and followed right along. It is thought to be Miss Lobb's ghost that haunts the upper rooms of the manor. Wispy ectoplasm has been seen to weave in and out of the ancient roof beams and a strange, deep voice is heard faintly calling as it echoes around the roof and upper chambers. These plaintive, strident calls apparently make anyone who hears them shiver with fear.

May is buried along with her sister Jenny, her father William, and his wife Jane in the grounds of nearby St George's Church in Kelmscott. Perhaps Miss Lobb cannot find May on the other side and through her constant calling and searching, she is attempting to intimidate anyone who witnesses her ghost. This apparition can remain dormant for many years before suddenly reappearing to haunt the upper chambers, beams and huge rafters of the mansion.

# The Half-finished Haunted House

## NYMPSFIELD, GLOUCESTERSHIRE

Mysterious Woodchester Park's salient feature today is a creepy, unfinished mansion with incomplete floors, fireplaces suspended in mid-air and staircases that lead to nowhere. It was purchased by William Leigh, a devout Roman Catholic, for the sum of £100,000 in 1844 and is now known at Woodchester Mansion.

After several false starts, Leigh engaged the services of a young architect named Benjamin Bucknall to replace Spring Park, the original Georgian country house situated on this estate, with a mansion in the Gothic style. Although incomplete, Bucknall's masterpiece exhibits a thorough understanding of medieval architecture with a startling blend of domestic and monastic styles. These features create a haunted atmosphere that fill some who view the mansion with dread. Rooms built for domestic purposes lie side-by-side with a perfectly proportioned chapel and the outside of the building is decorated with the insanely grimacing faces of many gargoyles.

William Leigh died in 1873, leaving behind a son who did not inherit his religious fervour. Many plans for the completion of the manor fell through due to lack of funds and the only building work finished after William's death was that of the drawing room, which was completed for a visit by Cardinal Vaughan in 1894.

After a number of changes of ownership, Woodchester Mansion, which is situated between Stroud and Nailsworth, was purchased by Stroud District Council with English Heritage providing 75 per cent of the monies needed. Emergency repairs were carried out but the completion of the mansion was considered too expensive a project. The mansion is now listed as a Grade I building which saves it from demolition.

In 1988 the Woodchester Mansion Trust was set up to preserve its present state and to arrange for courses in stonemasonry and architectural conservation to be made available

*A headless horseman haunts Woodchester Mansion.*

*A haunted room in Woodchester Mansion.*

*A creepy gargoyle at Woodchester Mansion.*

to students and the general public. With the help of grants, the trust has been able to complete the restoration of the grand staircase, the rainwater system, the West Range and the Clock Tower.

Local villagers have reported seeing a plethora of ghosts and creepy objects in and around the unfinished mansion, including a coffin hovering above a nearby lake which is thought to be that of a Dominican friar who committed suicide by drowning; a black dog; the ghost of a slightly built man standing in the doorway of the chapel; a headless horseman in Civil War clothes; and, in addition, pieces of stone and masonry mysteriously and dangerously flying through the air.

Perhaps all this spirit activity should not be surprising considering the fact that there were many accidents and eight deaths, one of which was a murder, during the construction of the building, which at one time employed up to 100 workmen. Woodchester Mansion is particularly scary on a dark, misty day with its staring, empty windows and bleak, unfinished interior. Ghost hunters are sure to get many thrills from visiting at a time like this.

# two

# OXFORDSHIRE ENTITIES

Oxfordshire, once part of the kingdom of Mercia, is 768 square miles in size and its name is derived from the Anglo-Saxon name 'Oxenaford', which translates as 'ford for oxen'. It was formed in the early tenth century and lies between the River Thames to the south, Gloucestershire to the west, the Chilterns to the east and the Midlands to the north. In addition, spurs of Oxfordshire run north to Banbury and south towards Henley-on-Thames.

Oxfordshire's crown jewel is Oxford University, which was founded in 1096, although it was not structured at that time in the collegiate manner that it is today. Oxfordshire was largely bypassed by the Romans and after the thirteenth century it became very prosperous through the trading of wool. Its scenic rolling hills, particularly those lying in the western part of the county, lend themselves to the rearing of sheep. The affluence that this produced during medieval times led to the construction of many magnificent 'wool' churches within its borders.

Several major cities and towns in Oxfordshire are within the designated area of outstanding natural beauty in the Cotswolds, including Oxford, Chipping Norton, Burford, Abingdon, Banbury and Didcot. Oxfordshire is noted for its fine castles, stately homes and farm buildings which are of great historical and architectural interest. These include Broughton Castle, Buscot Park, Great Coxwell Barn, Chastleton House and Kelmscott Manor.

The great antiquity of some of Oxfordshire's buildings indicates the likelihood of them harbouring visitors from the other side. Indeed, two of the examples above, Chastleton House (Chapter Seven) and Kelmscott Manor (Chapter One), are explored elsewhere in this book.

# Maude and the Monk

A door is opened; it creaks and its rusty hinges screech against the wood. It is the middle of a dark, winter night and the frost is just beginning to form on the bare trees outside. There is silence for a few moments and then comes the sound of rosary beads clattering against each other. The click-clack of the beads is accompanied by the barely audible pattering of bare feet across the cold, stone ground. A few minutes later a tapping is heard. It could be the wind knocking a tree limb against a window perhaps, but it is not. Moments later a door opens in response to this almost imperceptible sound. A hurriedly whispered conversation follows between two figures. They are that of a man who is swathed in long robes, and a small, young woman with a delicate face. The man clasps the woman to him and they embrace. The hood the man is wearing falls back to reveal his dark, handsome features. After their embrace the man and woman look fearfully around. They peer into the darkness trying to see if there are any witnesses to their rendezvous, but nothing stirs in the dark night except the mists that swirl around them as the temperature grows colder. The man draws the woman to him and kisses her passionately. She clings to him and together they slip inside. The door closes on a dark secret.

This assignation took place in a monastery in Weston-on-the-Green in Oxfordshire during the early medieval period. The woman with the rosary beads in this scene of illicit love was

*Weston Manor Hotel, once a haunted monastery.*

SITE OF THE
13TH. CENTURY GRANGE OF OSNEY.
A PART REMAINS. REBUILT 1587 AS
THE HOME OF HENRY LORD NORREYS.
SERVANT OF QUEEN ELIZABETH AND
AMBASSADOR TO FRANCE. BECAME THE
HOME OF THE BERTIES. EARLS OF
ABINGDON. RESTORED 19TH. CENTURY.

*A plaque at the Weston Manor Hotel.*

*Once the doomed lovers' trysting place.*

a nun called Maude. She had fallen for a young monk and broken her vows of chastity to be with him. On more than one occasion she had scampered the short distance from her room in a nearby convent, risking all to meet her lover. He, too, was taking a terrible chance by breaking his promise of celibacy, but youthful passion had overtaken all reason.

On this same night, before dawn, Maude returned to the convent. Nobody had noticed her absence and all was well. The following morning remorse consumed her and she prayed for the strength to renew her vows. But before very long, her passion returned and once again she slipped out of the convent, her bare feet numb against the cold stone as she hurried along the inky black corridors and out into the freezing air. But this time was different, for now she was being watched… this time would be the last time.

On this occasion Maude was followed as another nun had reported her absences and others at the monastery had been alerted of her secret visits. But Maude was unaware of any of this as she safely reached the bliss of her lover's arms. But a short time later the wooden door of the same monk's cell split with a thunderous crack as it was smashed in with an axe. The startled lovers froze in fear as they were discovered by the light of a candle held high. There they were caught *in flagrante delicto* and Maude, knowing the horrible fate that now awaited her, fainted dead away. A terrible retribution was at hand and one of these doomed lovers would soon die…

Now, many centuries later, the monastery is long gone. Numerous buildings have occupied this same spot and have been torn down and rebuilt over time. A Tudor mansion remains and today this building is the Weston Manor Hotel, and is within easy reach of the M40 motorway. It seems that Room 7 of this very beautifully appointed hotel has been built on the exact spot where Maude and her monk carried out their lovers' tryst. Maude lost her life shortly after the last meeting with her lover but did not rest in peace. Her spirit now belongs to the undead and has haunted the hotel on many occasions.

The Weston Manor Hotel with its gabled roof, baronial hall and wood-panelled walls could not, on first viewing, seem cosier. Its roaring log fires, surrounded by feather-cushioned easy chairs, are very inviting and surely nothing could disturb the guests as they relax at the hotel's fireside after a good meal, happily cradling their after-dinner brandies. But beware any visitor who has booked into Room 7. There have been many reports of Maude haunting this room which is, these days, decorated in dark oak panelling. Her spirit seems to be especially present in the bathroom, which was built earlier than the remainder of the Tudor building and is thought to date from the eleventh century.

There have been tales over the years of many strange experiences, including sensations of dread and of an unusually fierce heat developing through the night followed by the temperature plunging into extreme cold. On other occasions lights click on and off all by themselves. Although very few people have actually seen Maude's ghost, her presence has been felt many times. It is no wonder that poor Maude's soul cannot rest because of the terrible fate that befell her after her secret became known.

The monastery where her meetings with the young monk took place was the seat of the Abbot of Osney. One of the Abbot's tasks was to dispense justice and it was on his directive that Maude was sentenced to a horrible death.

The crackling wood had a delicious scent. Burning wood always does. The flames were reluctant to come to life at first and almost flickered out in the harsh winter gale that froze the monastery grounds. But eventually the flames took hold and soon a huge bonfire consumed the wooden stake to which Maude was tied. She prayed, as did all those witnessing this terrible scene. Tears streamed down her face as the heat from the fire rose but nothing could be done to save her and eventually she perished in the flames. This was the fate of all nuns who broke their vows in those barbaric times. Now Maude roams the rooms of the Weston Manor Hotel, perhaps looking for her lost love. It seems her passion is not spent.

# Squire Cobb's Revenge

## ADDERBURY, OXFORDSHIRE

The pretty town of Adderbury is mentioned in the *Domesday Book* and 1,000 years ago, when it was founded, it was called Eadburggebyrigg. It is situated 3 miles south of Banbury and 20 miles north of Oxford. The town is noted for its beautiful honey coloured Horton cottages, the diamond-patterned brick chimney stacks of its sixteenth-century houses, its two Roman archaeological sites and, perhaps most memorably, for its excellent teams of Morris dancers who have drawn audiences from miles around.

Its church, Saint Mary's, is one of the biggest and most architecturally important in the whole of Oxfordshire. The church dates back to the thirteenth century but was subsequently enlarged in both the fourteenth and fifteenth centuries.

Ghosts will feel very welcome here at St Mary's Church, which sports possibly the scariest gargoyles, grotesques and corbel heads in the whole of the Cotswolds, carved both inside and outside of its walls. In addition, the church is decorated with Green Men, griffins and chimeras (see the introduction of this book for a fuller description of these eerie church embellishments). There is an amazing corbel carved inside the church in the form of a terrifying ram's head with a semi-human face, and also a beast with human limbs to mention just a couple. In addition, a spectacular carved stone frieze runs around the outside of the church and incorporates just about every mythological creature, weird, ugly human and spooky animal ever imagined. These include a winged dragon, a mermaid with two tails, knights in battle, ladies in wimples and figures playing a plethora of musical instruments.

An Adderbury ghost hunter might think of the wild church carvings as an hors d'œuvre to the main course, which could perhaps be the well-documented haunting of Squire Cobb and his phantom horse and carriage which frequently comes thundering through the town. Squire Cobb is a familiar apparition to the inhabitants of Adderbury as he has made numerous ghostly appearances since his demise. He is said to haunt the town because his deathbed wishes were ignored. The nature of these wishes has been lost in the mists of time, but Squire Cobb must have been very unhappy about the whole episode because he repeatedly returns to remind the inhabitants and visitors of Adderbury of this great omission.

The apparition of Squire Cobb is seen atop his carriage whipping his horses on as they tear through the town at breakneck speed. When this coach meets a traffic obstacle it just passes right through it and then continues on, the horses galloping ever faster.

*Gargoyle from St Mary's Church, Adderbury.*

*Squire Cobb's grave in St Mary's Church.*

*Squire Cobb's ghost tears through this street.*

The snorting and whinnying of the protesting animals echoes loudly through the streets but when this happens, the spectre of Squire Cobb merely uses his whip on them with greater alacrity. Although this coach-and-four are visitors from another world, several witnesses have testified to the fact that the pounding of the horses' hooves makes the ground shake as these frenzied creatures gallop by.

# The Headless Sailor

## FARINGDON, OXFORDSHIRE

The screams were shattering; so loud and so horrible, in fact, that they could be heard on the other side of the town. Everybody who heard those terrible screams in Faringdon that day stopped what they were doing and wondered. They wondered who on earth could have produced such a sound and what had prompted that person to make it. It was hard to describe how agonised it was, it seemed more like the cry of a tortured animal than that of a human. But everyone who experienced that spine-chilling sound knew that it was a woman who had made it.

The year was 1702 and it was the mother of a young sailor, Hampden Pye, who had screamed. At the exact moment she uttered those shrieks she had been putting on her wrap in preparation for a visit to All Saints Church. At the time she was dressed in mourning clothes as she was about to attend the memorial service of her son, who had recently died a long way from home. Her husband, daughters and her other surviving son, Edmund, were with her when a macabre vision appeared only to her. This poor woman witnessed a phantom of her son and she would never be the same again.

It had all started before Hampden died. When he was small he had been his mother's favourite child. But later, when he was almost a man, he began to lose his way. His brother Edmund was a good lad and obeyed his mother's rules, but Hampden had become a great concern to both his parents. The boys' father, Sir Robert Pye, was lord of the manor of Faringdon and the duties that this post entailed meant that he had not always been present to administer a steadying paternal hand during Hampden's childhood.

The town of Faringdon is mentioned in the *Domesday Book* and received its charter in 1218. There is evidence of Roman occupation and bricks of this era can be seen in the cellar of the Crown Hotel. All Saints Church was built in 1086 but it was not until the twelfth century that a nave was added. In the following century a choir was also built. All Saints churchyard features prominently in the ghostly tale that is to follow.

Hampden went astray when his visits to the local taverns became more important to him than staying home. He drank a good deal and also showed much more interest in the women who frequented these taverns than his mother would have liked. Hampden had a friendly, outgoing personality and was particularly attractive to the wenches who visited the taverns as he was tall, good-looking and had money to jingle in his pockets. He was a little too friendly to all who crossed his path and that, perhaps, was his downfall.

Hampden and his mother had been very close when he was a child, but now that he was growing up she couldn't let him go. She was an assertive woman and had trouble acknowledging that her son had to make his own way as a man. She expressed her disapproval to Hampden about his drinking and womanizing but this only drove him further away. Sometimes his bed would be empty in the morning and he would stay away from home for three or four nights in succession.

Hampden's mother took to spying on him while he was carousing at the taverns and discovered he had formed a liaison with a barmaid. This devastatingly attractive young girl

*All Saints Church, Faringdon.*

was small with dark tresses and it was obvious that Hampden had fallen in love with her, for he had marriage on his mind.

A lord of the manor's son could not be allowed to marry a lowly barmaid, or so Hampden's mother thought, and she had her husband banish poor Hampden from England by forcing him to join the Navy.

The ship that Hampden joined was said to have been involved in a naval battle at Redondela, located in an inlet on the west coast of Spain. Hampden's ship suffered damage when it exchanged cannon fire with other ships from the French and Spanish fleet. Known as the Battle of Vigo, after another small town nearby, this engagement led to a stunning victory for the English and Dutch ships. There had been a plan devised by the English to take possession of silver treasure that was aboard the ships of their enemies. Most of the silver, however, had already been unloaded and taken to Segovia Castle for safekeeping. The French and Spanish fleet was decimated with as many as twenty warships, five galleons and more than a dozen trading vessels having been sunk, burned or captured. Despite missing out on the treasure, this battle was seen as a strategic victory by the English and Dutch allies and led to the signing of the Methuen Treaties. The changes brought about by these agreements ultimately added greatly to the prosperity of eighteenth-century Britain. However, poor Hampden Pye met his end during this battle when he was decapitated by cannon fire.

His grieving family was preparing for a memorial service when his spectre appeared to his mother. Hampden's apparition was a bloody sight for he held his gruesome, gory head in his hands. It is no surprise that his mother's screams could be heard for miles.

For many years afterwards Hampden's headless, restless shade, with his head still held in his hands, haunted the churchyard of All Saints. His spectre would usually materialise behind a gravestone when the mists swirled in the early dawn or very late at night. The people of Faringdon were so frightened by this haunting that the vicar of All Saints finally agreed to stage an exorcism with a bell, book and candle.

This ancient method of exorcism has been in existence since the ninth century and is one of the most powerful means of laying a ghost. In this case, the vicar of Faringdon first proclaimed the ghost of Hampden to be damned by the Devil; next the church bells were rung. Following this, a Bible was ceremoniously slammed shut and the many candles that had previously been lit were snuffed out. As the flames from the candles were extinguished, so it seems did the ghost of the wretched Hampden Pye, for his spirit was never to be seen again.

# Creepy Church Bells of Burford

## BURFORD, OXFORDSHIRE

King Charles II often stayed with his mistress, Nell Gwyn, in the George Hotel in Burford, Oxfordshire. He was usually there for Bibury race week. But the 'untouched by time' medieval town of Burford on the River Windrush has even more to boast of than this fact. It has a wonderful array of notable buildings, including the Great Almshouses that were founded by the Earl of Warwick in 1828, the fifteenth-century Lamb Inn and a Norman

*Burford Church, where phantom bells ring.*

*The ancient almshouses of Burford.*

'wool' church with its elegantly proportioned spire. It was in this church that a band of Roundhead mutineers were held before witnesing the beheading of three of their party by Oliver Cromwell. But it is Burford Church, the Elizabethan priory, now an Anglican convent, and the Old Rectory nearby that will be of interest to ghost seekers.

Typically, in the middle of a cold winter night, everything will be quiet until church bells would suddenly peal. They are heard by many in the town and seem to be coming from the vicinity of the church, but when the church's bells are examined, they are always still and unattended. However, the phantom bells are still heard ringing and nothing can be done to silence them.

On other occasions, the spectre of a monk has often been seen wandering around the convent, the rectory and the church. His cowl is pulled down over his face and he hurries to and fro as if in a very agitated state. It is hard to tell that he is not of flesh and blood and many times an unsuspecting visitor will step aside to make way for this frenzied ghost. As he passes he becomes almost transparent. It is only then that a startled passer-by will realise that this monk is a ghoul from another age.

Another visitor from the other side who roams the area is a hunter with a rifle. He has been seen striding about Burford, wearing clothes from an earlier era and aiming his rifle, making ready to fire. His ghost is said to be so realistic that those who happen to be in his line of fire when he takes aim are seen to duck to avoid being shot. However, the most frightening haunting of all in these parts has been known to happen on the road between Burford and Minster Lovell.

In past times, witnesses have reported that unwary men and women have, on a number of occasions, suddenly been swallowed up in a mysterious dark cloud. This cloud appears suddenly, scudding across the horizon and zooming up to a traveller at warp speed. When this person is enveloped in the cloud he or she has instantly been driven stark raving mad. No one knows what happens once an innocent soul enters this ectoplasmic atmosphere or what causes such a terrible affliction afterwards. Some say that those who experience this horrible event are taken on a trip to the fiery horrors of Hell; others say that all the spectres in the area gather to have sport with their victim. Perhaps nobody will ever know what happens inside this cloud because those who exit it, although still alive, are unable to give a description of their ordeal. They are left gibbering, incoherent wrecks who remain for the rest of their days as mad as March hares.

# three

# CREEPY COTSWOLD CASTLES

Fortified living spaces existed in the Stone Age when early man sheltered in caves and made defences to protect himself against invaders and wild animals. By the tenth century the Saxons constructed the first known castles with circular, wooden fences surrounded by a ditch. Castles were often built on hilltops, or if they were constructed in low-lying land they were surrounded by water, making them easier to defend. But castle construction really got going in this country after the Norman Conquest in 1066 when William the Conqueror invaded. He undertook a massive castle-building spree at this time in order to show his dominance over the inhabitants of Britain.

By the eleventh century, castle construction had moved along a little in sophistication and motte and bailey building was the norm. A motte, from the Norman-French word meaning turf, was a large mound of earth with a 'keep' or tower built on top. A 'bailey' referred to the outer wall of a castle and was usually made of wood.

In the twelfth century castles became even grander, with Norman keeps and curtain walls of stone. By the fourteenth century, courtyard castles sported turrets and were surrounded by moats. But the late fourteenth century saw the decline of castle construction and fortified, moated manor houses took their place.

During the barbaric times in which castles came into their own, much murder and mayhem took place. Thousands of casualties could be counted in the pitched battles that took place in and around them. Many invaders were drowned in the moats, others met a horrible death when boiling oil was tipped on them from cantilevered battlements and all manner of arrows, sling shots, stones and eventually cannons were used to defend the castle's walls. No castle was worth its salt unless it had a good torture dungeon for captured invaders and it is no surprise that just about every castle in the Cotswolds has a resident ghost or two to turn these magnificent buildings into the perfect tourist attraction.

# The Warwick Castle Wraiths

## WARWICK, WARWICKSHIRE

A terrifying scream is heard, followed several moments later by the sound of a body falling to the ground with a dull thud. A dagger clatters to the stone floor, the staccato sound of the heavy weapon echoing through the chamber. Blood gushes from a deep wound, quickly forming a crimson, sticky puddle. The victim of this terrible stabbing is Sir Fulke Greville, the owner of Warwick Castle. The year was 1628, and moments before, a terrible argument had erupted between Greville and his faithful servant Ralph Haywood. The gist of their conversation would most likely have been as follows:

'Master, have I not served you well these many years?' asks Ralph Haywood of Sir Greville, barely keeping a lid on his anger as he helps his master dress.

'Yes, Haywood, indeed you have – though if you do not hand me my jerkin this minute I should perhaps be obliged to give you a different answer.' Sir Greville languidly makes this reply in his usual arrogant tone. Haywood does not make a move but stares at his master, his face flushing with anger.

'What is this, Haywood?' Sir Greville asks this question when he realises that the atmosphere in the chamber has become charged with tension.

'It has come to my knowledge that your will and testament indicates nary a single coin shall be granted me upon your demise.' By now Haywood is incandescent with rage and spits this out through gritted teeth.

*Eerie Warwick Castle.*

*Warwick Castle by the River Avon.*

'What?' demands Sir Greville, 'How dare you presume to know the workings of my will and then have the audacity to upbraid me for their contents?'

'A slave I have been in your service for these many years. I have been at your bidding morning till night and have always given of my best – you have said of this yourself, master. For this I deserve more.' Haywood shouts these words but Sir Greville gives no quarter and replies even more arrogantly than before.

'Hand me my jerkin, slave that you are, and know your place. I warn that if you dare to challenge me again on this issue then you shall indeed receive nothing as I so desired – nothing but a good flogging that is.'

The seventy-four-year-old Sir Fulke Greville was notoriously stingy and his habitual parsimony had resulted in Haywood's mounting resentment. Upon hearing Sir Greville's last admonition, Haywood snapped and blind with rage he pulled out his dagger and plunged it into Sir Greville's chest.

As Sir Greville staggered back, he clutched at a wall hanging. This slowed his descent for a few moments and his eyes began to bulge as he tried to speak. But the words stuck in his throat and only a few strangled gasps issued from his mouth. Finally he crashed to the floor and as he did so, the front of his shirt turned bright red with dripping blood. Strange gurgling noises came from him as he writhed in agony on the cold stone. The pool of blood grew larger and slowly the gurgling sounds ceased.

Haywood's anger disappeared when he saw his master in such distress. His old servant instincts returned and he involuntarily reached out to help Sir Greville. But before he could touch him, the enormity of his deed filled him with horror. He pulled his hand away and gasped as a terrible remorse gripped him. In a sudden, impulsive move he seized the same dagger he had used only moments before. It dripped with gore, but Haywood seemed oblivious of this fact and struck himself, slitting his own throat in an instant. He sliced through his jugular vein and the blood gushed out of his body as water from a tap. Weakened, he first knelt beside his master and then with a despairing final gesture towards Sir Greville, he fell prostrate on the floor beside him. Within a few minutes he was dead.

Unfortunately, Haywood's master was not so lucky. Sir Greville clung to life but did so in agony as he subsequently contracted a terrible infection. His anguish-filled moans were terrible to behold and he suffered a pain-wracked death a few weeks later. He was buried nearby in the choir of St Mary's Collegiate Church, in a grand tomb bearing the following inscription:

Fulke Grevil
Servant to Queene Elizabeth
Councellor to King James
And Friend to Sir Phillip Sydney.
Trophaeum Peccati.

Sir Greville now haunts Warwick Castle's fourteenth-century Watergate Tower, or the Ghost Tower, as it is now known.

Warwick Castle must certainly make its ghosts feel at home since it has seen so many gruesome goings-on over the centuries, having been the site of beheadings, dungeon tortures, treachery, intrigue, murders and stabbings. Construction on Warwick Castle began in 1068 and it is thought to have been built on top of an old cathedral. The castle's position high on a cliff made it ideal for protecting the entire Midlands from attack. Strategically, Warwick Castle was in the perfect location to guard the Fosse Way and oversee any crossings of the River Avon.

It is said that fortifications were ordered to be built before construction was even begun on the castle in AD 914 by Ethelfleda, the daughter of Alfred the Great of Wessex and his wife Ealhswith. These fortifications were constructed to protect against the invading Danish Vikings.

After her husband Ethelred, the Earl of Mercia, died, Ethelfleda became an outstanding military leader and was pronounced 'Lady of the Mercians'. Today this would amount to being crowned Queen and Ethelfleda reigned for almost ten years. She died at Tamworth and was buried at St Peter's Church (which became St Oswald's Priory) in Gloucester. During her reign she created the street plan for Gloucester from reworked Roman ruins that is still in place to this day.

After the Norman Conquest, William the Conqueror, who built the castle, passed it on to the 1st Earl of Warwick. There was treachery and mayhem afoot when a later Earl of Warwick was attacked and captured in his very own castle and thrown into the dungeon until a huge ransom was paid by the Crown.

*The Earl of Cornwall was imprisoned here.*

The horrors continued when in 1312 Piers Gaveston, the first Earl of Cornwall, was captured by Guy de Beauchamp, the 10th Earl of Warwick, and accused of stealing royal treasure. He was imprisoned in the dungeon of the castle and beheaded in June of that year.

In addition to the terrifying torture dungeon in Caesar's Tower, with its dangling gibbet on display, the castle sports a gatehouse with two murder holes – which must be of interest to the ghosts in residence. These murder holes were handy for the defenders of the castle to shoot arrows through at their attackers or to pour boiling oil upon them.

Warwick Castle was involved in another evil intrigue when it became part of the Gunpowder Plot in 1605. Some of the conspirators in this plot to blow up the Houses of Parliament were hiding out in nearby Dunchurch waiting to discover if their plan had succeeded. When they received word that it had failed, they tried to make their escape as, by then, their identities were known. To this end they stole horses from the stables at Warwick Castle and fled. Their fate is told in a later ghost story in this book.

Warwick Castle had run through about twenty Earls of Warwickshire by the time it was acquired by a heritage group in the 1970s. Subsequently it was sold to the Tussauds Group in 1978 and was set up as a tourist attraction. It is now a scheduled ancient monument with a Grade I listing and was designated as 'Britain's Best Castle' by *The Good Britain Guide* in 2001.

Over the centuries the castle has witnessed so much blood, gore and intrigue that it is no surprise that it became a magnet for the many ghosts who inhabit its massive walls. An image of doom is said to roam the castle in the guise of the apparition of an enormous, vicious, black dog with bloodshot, glittering eyes and yellow fangs bigger and sharper than

*The Watergate Tower, where Sir Greville was stabbed.*

those of a cougar. This evil beast has been seen on many occasions haunting the turrets of the castle, drooling, snarling and scaring everyone in sight. This shape-shifting dog once took human form and is said to house the spirit of a servant named Molly Bloxham, who was employed as a dairy maid at Warwick Castle in the fifteenth century.

This servant would often short-change the local villagers when she sold them dairy products from the castle. These villagers were too intimidated by her reputation as a witch to protest but, in time, word reached the Earl of Warwick of her cheating ways and she was dismissed and punished. Her punishment enraged her as she was severely beaten in public. Afterwards, the humiliation of this made her bent on revenge. She called upon all her knowledge of the dark arts and cast a wicked spell. Several years later her spell worked for, when she died, her spirit entered that of the vicious black dog. This evil dog set about attacking those who had punished Molly Bloxham. It roamed the battlements and had such a realistic appearance that those who were haunted by it would swear beyond all that it was real.

For a long time the dog could not be caught but, finally, it was trapped in the Beauchamp Tower of the castle. Here, Molly Bloxham's spirit was exorcised from the dog. Afterwards this crazed animal set up a terrible baying and escaped its jailers by suddenly leaping from the open window of the tower, over the battlements and into the river below. The priests who had been involved in the exorcism raced down to the river to recapture the dog but no trace of it could be found. Now, from time to time, the spirit of the dog returns to haunt the castle; its howls rend the air and these sounds, together with its terrifying appearance, panting, hot breath and snarling growls send spine-chilling tingles through everyone who crosses its path.

Various other ghosts haunt this eerie castle, including a sobbing woman, soldiers marching back and forth, sounds of clanking chains and the cries of unhappy servants. Also, the ghost of a little girl is said to haunt the undercroft. This is the semi-basement of the castle and is a very creepy place indeed.

Over time, so many ghosts have gathered to haunt the castle that it has become the subject of research. The Kenilworth Bedroom was once the headquarters of Frances Evelyn 'Daisy' Greville, the Countess of Warwick, who supervised séances and other paranormal experiments there. Daisy Greville was an interesting character who lived from 1861 to 1938. Although married to Frances Greville (Lord Brooke), she was also the mistress of

*The creepy undercroft of Warwick Castle.*

*The ghost of Sir Greville emerges from his portrait.*

King Edward VII. In addition, she was something of a high-class courtesan and had affairs with a number of other men in the upper strata of society. However, Lady Brooke, as she was also known, was notoriously indiscreet about these affairs and gossip about her activities was all over London at that time. Her habit of openly discussing her private affairs earned her the nickname 'the Babbling Brook'. 'Daisy, Daisy', the famous music hall tune of the time, was inspired by and named after her. Apparently, Daisy Greville was a good medium because during the séance sessions that she arranged, contact was frequently made with the other side.

During the last dozen years catalogued records have been kept of the many hauntings at the castle and numerous mediums, dowsers and psychics who participated in this study have reported witnessing the same ghosts. These independent sightings have described, in great detail, the ghosts appearing and reappearing over time and have confirmed previous accounts down through the centuries. The assorted ghosts of Warwick Castle are so many and so varied that they have become celebrities in their own right. As a result, an episode of the television show *Most Haunted* was filmed at the castle in 2006.

Warwick Castle lies in the city of Warwick close to the M40 motorway and Birmingham International Airport and is open to the public. It receives many thousands of visitors every year who enjoy its many well-designed, exciting and educational attractions and this impressive building lies in a beautiful setting next to the River Avon. Warwick Castle should be at the top of the list for ghost seekers, who must be sure to visit the dungeon and the aforementioned Ghost Tower.

Typically, an unsuspecting visitor can be admiring Sir Greville's portrait and all will be well until Sir Greville's apparition suddenly materialises right out of his painted image. This hair-raising event has happened on numerous occasions and has turned more than one paranormal sceptic into a believer.

# The Captured King

## BERKELEY, GLOUCESTERSHIRE

The rustling sound could have been a rat scurrying down the stone steps to his prison, or perhaps it was his enemies approaching. King Edward II listened to the faint noises coming from outside his cell door but, after a few moments, his attention wandered for he was weary and he longed for an end to his suffering. He had reached a point at which he did not care what manner of end it would be – a release to freedom from his stinking cell, which was situated over the noxious fumes emanating from the 28ft-deep dungeon below, or an end which resulted in his execution. On this occasion the rustling subsided and all was quiet again.

The King settled back onto the cold stone bench that served as his bed. He had endured five months of captivity and torture and, strong as he was, the King knew that he could not go on in these conditions indefinitely.

His thoughts strayed to the events of the previous day. An attempt had been made to rescue him and it had almost succeeded, but when it was foiled he bitterly regretted its failure. His loyal followers had penetrated the castle to within a few feet of his cell before they were discovered. He heard their shouts as they were captured and beaten. Any hopes he had for freedom were dashed when his wife, Queen Isabella, who together with her lover Roger Mortimer was holding him prisoner, heard word of the rescue bid and called in her guards to thwart it. This caused the deposed King to realise that his life was in mortal danger. He knew that Queen Isabella would probably try to kill him soon. Loyal as his followers were, their failed rescue bid meant that they had unwittingly signed his death warrant, as Queen Isabella would not risk any more attempts to free the King.

The rustling sounds started up again. It was then that he realised his enemies were at hand. Suddenly the door of the cell burst open and the first figure that appeared was that of his jailer, Thomas Berkeley, the son-in-law of his wife's lover. Behind him were the hired killers, three men built like giants. Edward was still strong and when they attacked he fought with all his might, but he was no match for their onslaught and, after a terrible struggle, he was overpowered. One of these men held a red-hot poker and when he administered it to Edward, agonised screams echoed throughout the castle and could be heard for a great distance beyond.

The playwright William Congreve tells us in his play *The Mourning Bride* that hell hath no fury like a woman scorned and Queen Isabella was furious indeed. Her marriage to Edward was complicated, for although he sired four children with her, for most of their married life together he preferred consorts of his own gender. This must have been humiliating for Isabella, who was said to be a great beauty with a slender figure, pale skin and red hair. She married Edward when she was only twelve years of age and this marriage was an arranged, political union brought about to put an end to the wrangling between France and England over the possession of Gascony. The couple were married on 25 January 1308, a year after Edward had become King.

The King favoured several young men, but his most frequent companion was Hugh le Despenser and he continued his association with him despite entreaties from Queen Isabella to banish this rival to her affections. Eventually, Isabella took her own lover, Roger Mortimer. Together they assembled an army to depose Edward. They acquired six man-o'-war ships from Isabella's cousin, William I, Count of Hainault in Holland, in exchange for a marriage contract between William's daughter and Isabella's son.

Isabella and Roger Mortimer landed in Suffolk with an army of mercenaries and quickly defeated Edward, whose few supporters deserted without a fight. Next, they killed the entire Despenser family and captured Edward, forcing his abdication. Isabella and Edward's son, Edward III of England, ascended the throne, but because he was only fourteen at the time Isabella and Mortimer ruled as regents.

Isabella and Mortimer kept Edward II prisoner in Berkeley Castle for five months before ordering his execution. After his death, Edward's heart was placed in a silver box and interred in the high altar of St Peter's Chapel in Gloucester Cathedral. Members of the Berkeley family attended the service for the King that followed.

Disembodied screams have been heard many times in Berkeley Castle since the terrible day when the King was executed, 22 September 1327. They are thought to belong to the shade of Edward II as his restless soul relives the events of this gruesome time.

Berkeley Castle, established by Robert Fitzharding, Governor of Bristol, has been held by the same family since it was built in 1154. It was constructed after a directive was given by Henry II and its purpose was to defend England against the Welsh. The castle is located midway between Bristol and Gloucester in the village of Berkeley and commands far-reaching views over its 6,000 acre estate. These include vistas of the Berkeley Vale, the River Severn, a bowling green enjoyed by Elizabeth I, a deer park and terraced gardens which contain a pine grown from a tree cutting brought back from the Battle of Culloden in 1746 by the 4th Earl of Berkeley. The castle's construction is of a seldom-used design and is called a shell keep. It surrounds a central mound rather than being built on top of one. The keep is nearly circular, having one square tower and three semicircular ones.

Berkeley Castle has barely changed since it was built and has all manner of defences that can still be seen today. These include trip steps, arrow slits, cannons, murder holes and massive barred doors. The trip steps which lead to the dungeon are built with an irregular tread in order to make the marauding enemy stumble. This castle's many original and interesting features are well worth viewing. There is a fourteenth-century Great Hall with stained glass windows, a magnificent sixteenth-century wooden screen, a grand, long drawing room and an extensive minstrel's gallery. One of the castle's several ghosts could be that of the very last court jester, who fell to his death from this same minstrel's gallery.

In 1645 Berkeley Castle was captured by the Parliamentarian Colonel Thomas Rainsborough after a siege that led to considerable damage. The Berkeley family were only allowed to continue their ownership of the castle when a promise was extracted from them to never repair the walls that had been breached by cannon fire from the roof of the Church of Saint Mary the Virgin nearby. These walls remain in ruin to this day, with the exception of a low barrier built for the safety of visitors. In the twentieth century the castle was repaired and slightly altered by the 8th Earl Randall, who ordered a porch be constructed that blended well with the Gothic style of the existing architecture.

Isabella and Mortimer retained their power for only three further years after Isabella's son took the throne on 25 January 1327. Upon reaching the age of eighteen, Edward III asserted his independence. When he did this, Parliament was called into session in Nottingham and Roger Mortimer was condemned without trial and thrown into the Tower. Isabella pleaded for Mortimer's life with the words, 'Fair son, have pity on gentle Mortimer', but he was hanged at Tyburn on 29 November 1330 and all his estates were returned to the Crown. Edward III spared Isabella and she retreated to Castle Rising in Norfolk. She died on 22 August 1358 and was buried in her wedding dress at the Franciscan church in Newgate. King Edward's heart was buried with her.

Edward II's apparition returned more recently when a ghoulish re-enactment of his funeral procession took place before a startled and terrified band of friends who were walking past the castle after a night of revelry in a local public house. Sceptics dismissed their description of what happened next on that dark, misty night as the result of imbibing too much alcohol. However, when interviewed separately every member of this group gave an identical, detailed description and it was impossible not to believe their account.

All of these young people had walked past the castle on numerous other occasions without incident and on this night were proceeding in their usual carefree manner. But this time the entire group stopped dead in their tracks when a massive, studded, wooden door opened up from a wall of the castle with an ominous, spine-tingling creak. Everybody then gasped and clutched each other in fear as a cadre of soldiers on horseback, clearly from another era, slowly exited the castle and came towards them. These were followed by hundreds of soldiers on foot who marched past the group in formation as they followed those on horseback. Next, accompanied by dozens of monks, their cowls draped over their faces, a dolorous cortege followed with a dray carrying a flag-covered coffin.

Gradually it dawned on this group of friends that they were watching the funeral procession of Edward II as it made its way to Gloucester. These witnesses described many details that were corroborated when compared to historic accounts of the actual event. The group of friends were left shivering in fear and awe as the realisation came upon them that the vivid image before their eyes was a ghostly recreation of an event that had actually taken place a little over 700 years earlier.

*four*

# EERIE INNS

It was the Romans who instituted drinking establishments and these taverns first provided ale to their customers over 2,000 years ago. But these taverns disappeared with the decline of the Roman Empire and it wasn't until the religious pilgrimages of early medieval times that drinking inns were re-established. The massive number of people involved in these religious travels put a severe strain on the monasteries that had previously provided sustenance to wayfarers and it was monks who opened the first inns.

Later, the beginnings of the Industrial Revolution saw a big growth in coaching inns. By this time, monks were no longer involved in their management. As commerce expanded it became apparent that excellent roads were needed for the speedy transport of goods. Toll roads helped pay for the improvements that followed and in 1657 the first coaching route between Chester and London was put into service. Within the next 100 years, most major cities and towns had their own routes established.

The need for frequent stops for coach drivers, allowing their horses and passengers to rest and find sustenance, created a demand for coaching inns. Coaches stopped every twenty miles or so and many inns were built to take advantage of this fact.

In those days, coaching inns fulfilled a number of functions and became centres for business negotiations, auctions, trade and the storage of goods. There was also much drunkenness associated with them as consuming too much alcohol was not condemned nearly as much as it is today.

The image of coaching inns has become romanticised in this day and age. It usually portrays a speeding coach, a team of wide-eyed horses, flanks steaming and nostrils flared, galloping along a deserted country track until the coach arrives at an inn. The alighting passengers are greeted by the stout, bewhiskered landlord who sits these weary travellers down by a roaring fire and serves them overflowing pints of ale accompanied by a side of beef, surrounded by roast potatoes and dripping with gravy.

But travellers beware – for on that deserted track often waits a highwayman who is not made of flesh and blood, or perhaps upstairs in that cosy lodging at the inn a spirit from the undead lurks, for ghosts like coaching inns too!

*The Ram Inn, the most haunted building in Britain.*

*The ghost of a woman rose from this grave.*

# The Ram Inn Poltergeists

## WOTTON-UNDER-EDGE, GLOUCESTERSHIRE

Creepy tales of mysterious deaths, exorcisms, devil worship, excavated skeletons, apparitions, a suicide and evil spirits make the atmosphere of the former Ram Inn at Potters Pond, Wotton-under-Edge, so laden with spookiness and doom that many visitors are forced to flee before they have spent more than a short time inside this building.

Once a public house dating back to the twelfth century, the Ram Inn was originally built on the site of a pagan burial ground. This explains why there is credence to the claim of it being the most haunted house in Britain. This building is now in private ownership but visitors are sometimes allowed to tour its dark interior. These visitors frequently return with tales of terror.

The Ram Inn, often wreathed in mist, sprawls several feet below the road looking for all the world like the half-sunken hulk of a ship-wrecked galleon from the Spanish Armada. It sports a jigsaw puzzle of added-on wings and mouldering, dimly-lit windows. Inside, a warren of freezing rooms are cluttered with strange antiques, yellowing memorabilia, dressing tables heaped with religious objects, portraits of subjects with staring, haunted eyes and the eerie, stuffed heads of long-dead animals.

The Ram Inn is typical of other buildings of this era in that its small, leaded windows let in very little light. The fact that this building is situated in a hollow below the road further intensifies its dank atmosphere and a feeling of foreboding permeates the entire

*Ghouls haunt the Bishop's Room in the Ram Inn.*

building. It is no surprise, therefore, that the odd ghost or other entity that goes bump in the night might appear to haunt its occupants from time to time. But at the Ram Inn, the ghosts appear in their dozens and seem to be tripping over themselves to give any visitors a thoroughly good scare. There are so many, in fact, that it is necessary to describe their visitations room by room.

This author was given a tour of the Ram Inn by its current owner Mr John Humphries, who has lived in the pub, which is currently a private residence, for almost thirty years. The tour began on the upper level.

## The Bishop's Bedroom
Mr Humphries led the way into a dusty bedroom that contained twin single beds covered in decaying candlewick bedspreads. The carpets were tattered and threadbare and the smell of mould added to the sense of unease and gloom that enveloped the room.

Mr Humphries indicated the fireplace in this room where black magic and satanic artefacts had been discovered. Apparently, two visitors who spent the night here were so scared by a haunting of the satanic spirits that they fled in terror. Many of the visitors who have stayed here have, subsequently, had to be repeatedly exorcised by a religious leader.

Mr Humphries talked of three other ghosts who have tormented visitors to the Bishop's Bedroom. He described the shade of an elderly shepherd who, together with his dog, has been seen sadly wandering around and around the single beds, presumably looking for lost sheep.

A Cavalier in battle dress also appears and disappears by charging through walls as if he were about to attack the enemy.

Many encounters have been reported by Mr Humphries of an incubus and succubus who feed on a mortal person's life force. A number of visitors who encountered these spirits have had to seek medical attention afterwards.

## The Witch's Room
Our host on the tour seemed unwilling to enter this room himself and talked about the ghosts who haunt it from the position he took up in the doorway. Apparently, the spirit of a woman accompanied by her cat has been seen by visitors to this room on numerous occasions. This woman could quite possibly have been a witch in her mortal life, as it is well-known that witches often used cats – known as familiars – to carry out their spells and curses.

## The Beaufort Room
An illuminated ectoplasm has been seen in this room and, according to Mr Humphries, this entity has been known to move with great speed.

## The Attic
The ghost of a female, most likely a servant, has been seen here at night. The shade carries out domestic chores for several hours at a time. This room had a particularly clammy atmosphere and rampant damp made the air rank.

*Satanic ritual artefacts were found here.*

## The Kitchen

Mr Humphries indicated the site of an ancient grave here and explained that that it had been excavated before he took up residence in the building. Some of the original flagstones had been removed and the excavation is still open, revealing a deep hole dug in the earth beneath the building. The body of a woman and child were discovered in this excavation and were thought to have died in a ritual sacrifice.

Apparently, the ghost of a woman rises up out of this grave from time to time and has been seen sadly weeping.

## The Barn

This large edifice adjoins the house and is cluttered with mouldering antiques that Mr Humphries purchases from sales all over the county. A narrow path threads through the stacks of old paintings, lamps, tables, wardrobes and other paraphernalia. The temperature here seemed even colder than elsewhere in the building and the air was so clammy that the horror associated with these spirits seemed almost palpable. Sometimes, apparently, the ghosts seen in the other rooms of the Ram Inn congregate here in the barn, which perhaps accounts for its chilling atmosphere.

Any brave souls who elect to spend a few hours or a night at the inn looking for a ghost encounter are almost guaranteed a visitation by one or other of these unnerving entities. Horrified visitors often leave in the middle of the night or the next morning, shaking with fear, and report that nightmares plague them for months afterwards.

# The Creepy Ragged Cot

## MINCHINHAMPTON, GLOUCESTERSHIRE

The charming, but creepy, Ragged Cot is a seventeenth-century inn tucked beside almost 600 acres of beautiful Cotswold land administered by the National Trust. This land is known as Minchinhampton Common and sits close to the small market town of Minchinhampton.

It overlooks some of the finest views in the English countryside between the Frome and Nailsworth valleys. There are important archaeological remains on this common, including the Bulwarks, which are part of an Iron Age defence system, and the long barrow known as Whitfield's Tump.

Perhaps this ancient burial mound is the source of the weird noises that are regularly heard by visitors to the Ragged Cot. In addition, there are said to be many ghoulish inhabitants of this inn, including a former landlord named Bill Clavers who, in 1760, murdered his wife and child in a drunken stupor.

The Ragged Cot's architecture is perfectly suited to a ghostly encounter with its stone walls and Gothic side windows which make it look akin to a country church. Today, it is a great place to buy a pint and a plate of 'pig's twigs' (trotters) and to find that dogs and Wellington boots are welcome.

This pub and restaurant has been tastefully remodelled but has retained many of its original features and offers delicious food. It is a good base from which to hike across Minchinhampton Common, to visit other lovely towns in the Cotswolds and to enjoy a little ghostly action at the same time.

In this very same building, on a dark, misty winter's night more than 200 years ago, Bill Clavers, the innkeeper of that time, made up his mind to rob the stagecoach that stopped

*The creepy Ragged Cot from the road.*

close by at midnight on its way to London. To give himself courage Clavers filled up with plenty of rum. He then collected his loaded pistols and drunkenly left his bedroom to carry out his plan. His wife tried to stop him and pleaded with him to give up this dangerous notion. She was holding her tiny child in her arms as they argued. Impatiently, Bill Clavers made a move towards the stairs but his wife clung to him, pulling him back. He flared up in an alcohol-fuelled temper and pushed his wife and child angrily aside. But he pushed too hard and, to his horror, they tumbled head-first down the steep staircase. Mad with drink, he dashed out of the house and carried out his plan to rob the midnight stagecoach.

When he returned to the Ragged Cot he found his wife and child dead at the bottom of the stairs. In a panic, he put their bodies in a trunk. Meanwhile, two constables picked up Clavers' trail at the scene of the hold-up and tracked his footsteps in the snow back to the inn. With their pistols at the ready, the constables forced an entry and encountered Clavers. They aimed their pistols at him and he raised his in return. But a moment before any firing took place, the air in the room suddenly dropped in temperature. It seemed to paralyze all in the room. Next, a moaning sound was heard drawing everybody's attention to the trunk. At that moment, to everybody's horrified amazement, the ghost of the innkeeper's wife, with her child in her arms, rose up out of the trunk, walked across the room and climbed the stairs.

*The ghostly staircase of the Ragged Cot.*

*Another view of the haunted Ragged Cot.*

Clavers fell back, his eyes staring and glazed. The moaning could be heard from the upper room of the inn. Clavers, overcome with fear and guilt, began to sob. When the constables recovered from what they witnessed, they took Clavers into custody. This time he offered no resistance.

The next day the body of Clavers' wife and child were found, not in the trunk where they had been placed but at the bottom of the stairs.

Bill Clavers' trial took place at the Gloucester Assizes and, after being found guilty, he was sentenced to be hanged until dead. This poor wife and her baby can be heard wailing pitifully at the inn, especially on stormy nights. Their sad cries echo through the inn after midnight and give listeners many a chill.

# The King's Head Horrors

## CIRENCESTER, GLOUCESTERSHIRE

The haunted King's Head Hotel is located in Cirencester and recent excavations have been carried out under its foundations revealing remains of a Roman road and artefacts.

When the Roman army occupied Britain, their soldiers were notoriously brutal. Perhaps the unspeakable tortures this army inflicted upon the local citizens before executing them accounts for the myriad spirits whose lost souls wander Cirencester to this day.

Cirencester was an important Roman settlement and at the time of this occupation was the second largest city in Britain. An amphitheatre situated to the south-west of the town has yet to be fully excavated and there are many more Roman ruins nearby, including those of Chedworth and Withington.

Wool manufacturing was well established during Roman times in Corinium, as Cirencester was then called. The town was fortified in the fifth or sixth century; the '-cester' part of the name indicating that it was a fortress. The minster church of

Cirencester was built some time between the ninth and tenth century but was razed by Augustinian monks in the twelfth century and replaced by the abbey church, which was dedicated in 1176.

Archaeologists have discovered a 2,000-year-old Roman high street below the Corn Hall and the King's Head pub. A baker's oven, the walls of shops and many artefacts such as Roman bronze coins, a perfume bottle and other domestic objects have been excavated.

The occupants of the King's Head have reported terrified wailing, perhaps from the spectre of a citizen tortured by Romans and, in addition, the apparition of a monk who scared a member of the staff so badly that this terrified employee resigned from her job. Several visitors to the King's Head, which dates back to the sixteenth century and was once a coaching inn, have been scared by the figures of ghosts who have appeared and disappeared with alarming speed. Finally, another ghastly apparition which takes the form of a cavalier has also been seen by members of staff, which has left them quaking in their shoes.

# The Banshee of Banbury Cross

## BANBURY, OXFORDSHIRE

Ride a cock horse to Banbury Cross,
See a Fyne lady ride on a white horse.
With rings on her fingers and bells on her toes,
She shall have music wherever she goes.

This well-known nursery rhyme, often chanted when the town of Banbury is mentioned, is thought to be over 200 years old. The 'Fyne' in the second line probably refers to one of the daughters of Lord Saye and Sele, a member of the Fiennes family who lived in Broughton Castle close by.

The Saxons who colonised the west banks of the River Cherwell are responsible for the origins of Banbury as we recognise it today, but human settlement of this area goes back much farther. The Romans invaded this region and recent excavations in Banbury have revealed evidence of an Iron Age community. Many domestic artefacts were discovered in and around the remains of a circular house on the site in Henneff Way, including pottery shards and milling stones.

There have been several crosses in Banbury throughout history but only one remains and is located in the centre of four roads. These are Warwick, Shipston-on-Stour and Oxford Roads, and Banbury High Street. This cross was built to mark the marriage of Victoria Mary Louisa, Queen Victoria's daughter, to Friedrich Wilhelm of Prussia in 1858.

This region was invaded by the Danes in AD 913 when they pillaged the entire north of Oxfordshire. But perhaps Banbury owes its existence to their occupation, because the Danes were well-known for their creation of market towns. The market place in Banbury is triangular in shape and is of a typical Danish design. Market days are now held twice a month with a farmer's market held every last Friday.

*Banbury Cross, close to a haunted hotel.*

Banbury boasts several eerie inns, but perhaps the most famous is the Whately Hall Hotel which dates back to 1632. This fine former coaching inn is built of stone and is close to Banbury Cross. Set in beautiful gardens, this hotel retains many of its original seventeenth-century details including oak-panelled and beamed corridors, stone-built fireplaces, secret staircases and a priest's hole.

Many visitors have reported hauntings by a ghost known as Father Bernard. This spectre provides quite a contrast to the typical lost souls whose sad wailings echo through many an eerie inn. Father Bernard is that rare breed of spook – a jolly ghost. He jauntily hurries along the corridors of the Whately Hall Hotel, sometimes humming but more often smiling and chuckling all the way.

After Henry VIII's Reformation, priests were the subject of religious persecution and were summarily hunted down and captured. Many people must have wanted to help these unfortunate men because numerous priests' holes have been found in medieval buildings. These well-hidden refuges were reached by secret staircases such as those in the Whately Hall Hotel.

Perhaps Father Bernard's shade is jubilant because he was never discovered by his persecutors during his lifetime, and was allowed to die a natural death. Why his spirit stays on to haunt the hotel is a mystery, but he seems quite at home and happy as he scampers around. He favours going up and down the stairs quite frequently, it seems, because he has been encountered there many times.

He has also been seen in the hotel grounds with his monk's cowl pulled down over his face. When Father Bernard is outside he is even more joyful and has been seen skipping

*Whately Hall Hotel where priests hid.*

*Escape route for priests in the Whately Hall Hotel.*

and hopping as he passes right through trees and shrubs. Sometimes his giggles and chortles wake up the hotel guests but his laughter is infectious and no complaints have been received.

Those who come face to face with this frolicsome phantom are said not to be frightened at all. Some are curious and move towards his ethereal figure when they encounter it. On these occasions, Father Bernard chooses to disappear instantly. Other visitors have a different reaction when they meet him. They stop in their tracks and are confused, unable to decide if he really is from the other side. However, it quickly becomes apparent that Father Bernard is not of this world when he walks right through these hotel visitors and chuckles to himself as he continues on his merry way.

# The Spectre of Stow

## STOW-ON-THE-WOLD, GLOUCESTERSHIRE

Today, any visitor to the 500-year-old Kings Arms Hotel in Stow-on-the-Wold would see a tranquil, picture-perfect scene. Nestled between other ancient buildings in the cobble-stoned market place, this half-timbered former coaching inn is so camera-ready that it could be mistaken for a film set. In fact, it was used as one in 1970 when the BBC shot an adaptation of Thomas Hardy's *The Mayor of Casterbridge* in and around it.

Many modern-day visitors have enjoyed this lovely inn's hospitality and its quaint accommodation, complete with atmospheric, perfectly-preserved Elizabethan décor. The fine cuisine and ten bedrooms offered by this posting inn, some of which are tucked in the eaves of the roof, make it a much sought-after hostelry.

The townspeople and visitors strolling by this handsome Tudor building on a typical, bustling market day with the sun shining and birds singing would therefore find it hard to imagine the gruesome, bloody scenes that took place on this very spot in 1646.

It was then that the Royalist army marched through Stow-on-the-Wold on their way to join up with King Charles I in Oxford. They were attacked by Parliamentary troops and the fighting was so deadly that the streets of Stow were said to be awash with blood, and the legend has it that ducks were able to paddle in the gory pools that formed in the narrow streets branching off from the market place. One of these alleys is named Digbeth Street, and many think that this name is derived from 'duck's bath'.

It was in this final battle of the Civil War that the Royalists were soundly beaten and more than 1,000 of them were taken prisoner and held in the eleventh-century St Edward's Church, which is also situated in the market square. The nearby St Edward's Hall houses an exhibition of Civil War artefacts in addition to the public library.

In medieval times, Stow-on-the-Wold was a very prosperous wool town and its enormous market square, which was created in 1107, could accommodate 20,000 sheep. Often that same number were sold in just one day. The streets leading from the market place were designed to be exceptionally narrow in order to better control any escaping sheep.

The Kings Arms Hotel was visited by King Charles I in May 1645, a year before the battle, and it has not changed much since that day. Its window and door frames are a

*Ghosts of soldiers haunt the Kings Arms Hotel.*

*Digbeth Street, where blood flowed.*

*The haunted Kings Arms Hotel.*

little crooked these days, but that is to be expected of a building of this antiquity. In the meantime, this inn has also acquired several ghosts. Late at night, sad, wailing cries are sometimes heard and no one can explain their origin. These wailings and sobs are thought perhaps to be coming from the ghosts of those soldiers who met their end in the Civil War battle that took place only a few paces away.

Several ghosts and strange entities visit the Kings Arms so frequently that their presence has become quite commonplace to the staff who work there. One particularly regular otherworldly visitor is a very lifelike woman in Victorian dress. She is said to wear a high-necked, white lace blouse, caught at the throat with a cameo brooch, and featuring leg-of-mutton style sleeves. Her skirt is made of black silk and worsted bombazine, which was a very commonly used fabric during the Victorian era. Her grey tresses are piled up in a 'cottage bun' style hairdo of the period. She carries a dainty, lace-embroidered handker-chief, is prosperous looking and wears expensive jet jewellery.

This Victorian spectre manages to fool guests every time she appears because she seems so real. She has a habit of turning lights on and off without touching the switches and of making doors open of their own accord. When astonished guests describe these manifes-tations to the staff, they are generally met with the same reply: 'The old lady ghost has probably been up to her tricks again'.

This ghost is apparently fascinated by the television which is often on in the public lounge of the hotel and frequently sits alongside other unsuspecting guests when they are viewing programs. She takes no notice of anyone around her and later these guests are willing to swear on all that they own that this grey-haired elderly ghost is real, albeit wearing weirdly old-fashioned clothes, until she vanishes from a room with no exit other than the one they have in view. It is only when the Victorian ghost lady disappears that these terrified guests realise that they have been enjoying their favourite programs with a spook from another dimension.

# five

# CADAVEROUS COTSWOLD KINGS AND QUEENS

It is thought that the first King of England was Offa of Mercia, who designated himself as such in AD 774, although conflicting accounts throughout history cast some doubt on this fact. The English kingdom was formed in a more permanent fashion in AD 954 by Eadred and was further bolstered when Wales became part of Britain in 1284. In 1301 Edward of Caernarfon was invested as the Prince of Wales and since then every eldest son of a British monarch, bar one, has carried the same title.

The earlier monarchs seem to have been blessed with much more colourful names than those who were crowned following medieval times. A selection of these royals, not known for their self-effacement, had such titles as Edward the Magnificent, Edgar the Peaceable, Athelstan the Glorious, Edward Longshanks and Richard the Lionheart; Oliver Cromwell was known as Old Ironsides and, of course, there was Ethelred the Unready – apparently Ethelred could never quite get to a battle on time.

When Queen Elizabeth I of England died in 1603, England and Scotland were united under one monarch, King James, who titled himself King of Great Britain. .

A number of British monarchs, kings and queens alike, have met gruesome ends in the Cotswolds and their ghosts seem to want to linger on, ready to scare anybody who encounters them, as the following stories in this chapter will show.

# The Headless King

## PAINSWICK, GLOUCESTERSHIRE

Painswick, near Stroud, is situated on a high promontory between two valleys and overlooks a number of old mills situated on a stream. King Charles I was quartered in this town, at the Court House, when he ordered the Siege of Gloucester to begin in 1643. His ghost haunts the Court House with many sightings having been recorded throughout the years. His ghostly form appears and disappears with great frequency and there have been numerous descriptions of this event and of his tortured moans.

King Charles, in his arrogance, thought it would be an easy matter to overcome the resistance of the Parliamentary forces who were holding out in the city of Gloucester during the First Civil War (some historians divide the English Civil War into three parts). The King reached Gloucester on 1 August 1643 and soon 30,000 of his Royalist troops surrounded the city. But the cannon fire they directed at the fortified walls had little effect and only fifty of those defending Gloucester were lost.

When news of the attack reached London, a newly recruited army of 15,000 men was dispatched to save Gloucester. When King Charles discovered that these troops were on their way, he withdrew his men. This was fortunate for the city as only three barrels of gunpowder remained unused at that time.

After the second round of the Civil War in 1648, which he also lost, King Charles was tried for high treason and other crimes. No previous monarch had ever been brought to trial and King Charles refused to enter a plea, saying that no court had jurisdiction over a monarch. However, he was convicted and sentenced to execution. When a Parliamentarian read his conviction, King Charles tried to stop him by poking him with his cane. As he did so, the silver top of this cane fell to the ground but nobody would pick it up. After several minutes the King bent down to retrieve it himself. This was thought to be a pivotal moment that showed the divine monarch bowing before human law.

At his execution, King Charles wore two thick shirts to ward off the freezing weather. This was done so that the crowd would not mistake any shivering on his part as fear. In his last moments the King said a prayer: 'I shall go from a corruptible to an incorruptible Crown, where no disturbance can be'. He then put his head on the masked executioner's block and was beheaded with a clean stroke as a great moan went up from the crowd. Several witnesses were said to have seen the King's spirit leave his body and hover over his corpse. King Charles was buried on 7 February 1649 inside the same vault as Henry VIII in St George's Chapel, Windsor Castle.

In addition to the haunting of the Court House by King Charles, the ghosts of his Cavaliers have been seen many times in the gardens and surrounding grounds as they make their elaborate preparations for battle. These ghosts materialise and dematerialise constantly, striking fear into the hearts of any witnesses who may be present, as they slowly don all their accoutrements of war. King Charles' ghost also haunts another location, which is described in the next story.

# The Chavenage Shades

## TETBURY, GLOUCESTERSHIRE

Shortly after King Charles I's execution, which took place in the Palace of Whitehall, his ghost was seen at Chavenage House. This perfectly preserved Elizabethan manor near Tetbury is today open to the public and should be on the top of any serious ghost hunter's list to visit as it is haunted not only by King Charles, but also by several other entities.

During the time of the Civil War, Chavenage was the home of the Parliamentarian Nathaniel Stephens. His distant cousin, Oliver Cromwell, made a special visit to his house to persuade Stephens to authorise the execution of Charles I. The room that was designated for this visit, the magnificent Tapestry Room, is now known as the Cromwell Room and a visit to it is like a walk back in time.

This author was privileged to receive a warm welcome and an informative and entertaining private tour of Chavenage House by Mrs Rona Lowsley-Williams. Her family currently owns this historically important estate and she kindly pointed out where all the ghosts that haunt this house had appeared.

Mrs Lowsley-William's expertise in the showing of the house is apparently only rivalled by that of her husband, David, who has raised the level of the stately home tour to a high art. The entire Lowsley-Williams family pitch in with great energy and resourcefulness to maintain Chavenage House in an excellent state of repair, helped only by grants from English Heritage.

*Engraving of ghostly Chavenage House.*

*Cromwell's bedroom,*
*Chavenage House.*

The guidebook for Chavenage House contains excellent information with a chronology of the mansion beginning in the year 1000, and will be of interest to those who search out the paranormal as it also makes several references to the resident ghosts, including that of a 'grey lady'.

During the Second World War, Mrs George Lowsley-Williams, an ancestor of the present-day family, was working as a lady-in-waiting to Princess Marie Louise, whose mother was the third daughter of Queen Victoria. During the wartime evacuations from London, the Princess frequently stayed at Chavenage House and in her book, *My Memories of Six Reigns,* she tells of her encounters with a ghost when she was visiting. She was repeatedly haunted by an entity that made a habit of noisily opening and closing doors. In addition, the Princess's maid described seeing a woman in an old-fashioned dress as she walked past her and into a room occupied by the Princess, who was at the time lying on her bed resting. The maid saw this 'grey lady' bend over the Princess and noticed her beautiful hands and lace ruffles at her wrist. A moment or two later, this entity quietly withdrew and faded away.

Perhaps the ghosts feel at home here because the house seems so completely untouched by time. Chavenage has had only two owners – the Stephens and the Lowsley-Williams families – since it was rebuilt as a Tudor mansion in 1576. Almost nothing has changed in the house since that era and it contains many Elizabethan furnishings and artefacts that are completely intact and fascinating to view.

Although it was rebuilt by the Stephens family, Chavenage House boasts even earlier beginnings, dating from the ninth century when it was the meeting place of the Hundred Court and later when it was owned by Princess Goda, the sister of Edward the Confessor. The Stephens family, who had come over with William the Conqueror from France, first gained possession of the house in 1564. At the time, this prominent family also owned estates in Lypiatt, Cherington, Lyegrove and Sodbury. After obtaining the house, the family largely tore down the existing medieval building and constructed a porch and two wings. This followed the design of a typical Elizabethan manor house of the era. Reclaimed ecclesiastical glass was obtained from the decommissioned churches and monasteries of the

*Chavenage House
as it is today.*

surrounding area and broken-up timbers from naval galleons were gathered from the River Severn for the construction of the roof. In 1576, Edward Stephens and his wife Joan, carved their initials above the front door of Chavenage House when the work was completed.

In 1648 Edward's descendent, Nathaniel Stephens, succumbed to the intense pressure put upon him by Cromwell to agree to the execution of King Charles. However, shortly thereafter he bitterly regretted this decision. Subsequently, Stephens' daughter Abigail laid a curse on her father for bringing the family name into disrepute through his actions. It is said that Stephens was soon taken ill and died only four months after the demise of King Charles. His death is thought to have been hastened by his daughter's curse and the remorse he felt for having agreed to the King's execution.

After his death, mourners gathered at Nathaniel Stephen's funeral but were horrified at the events that unfolded before their eyes. Just before the service began, a strange chill enveloped everybody. The mourners tried to wrap their clothing more tightly around themselves but could not do so as they were unaccountably paralyzed. Next, they were terrified when a spectral coach materialised before them, pulled by a team of black horses. Out of the coach stepped King Charles. At first the mourners did not recognise him because he was headless. But when they realised he was wearing the Royal livery, they understood it was the King. Many of the mourners fainted at this grisly sight and those that did not again tried to flee.

However, they were unable to do so because of their paralysis and cried out in fear as the next horrible apparition appeared. This was the ghost of Nathaniel Stephens, who climbed out of his coffin, shook off his shroud and walked over to the apparition of the coach and six horses. Stephens and the headless King Charles climbed into the coach and it took off at high speed. However, before the horses had galloped more than 100yds along the cobbled drive, the coach and all in it burst into flames. Terrible, tortured screams accompanied this event. When the flames finally died down, the mourners were released from their paralysis and ran screaming in fear from the scene.

Chavenage House is open to the public between May and September on Thursdays, Sundays and certain Bank Holidays from 2 p.m. to 4.30 p.m. Groups are welcome by

# Blood at Blackfriars Priory

## GLOUCESTER, GLOUCESTERSHIRE

First there was the thudding of footsteps, as if someone was running very fast. Soon this sound was accompanied by terrifying screams so horrible that everybody who heard them stopped in their tracks. The noise seemed to be coming from the nave of the church in the priory. The footsteps drew closer and next, the heavily-breathing figure of a monk appeared. At first he seemed real, but then a closer look showed him to be a spectre. His form was not human for at times it was possible to look right through him. His hood had fallen back to reveal that he had a serious head wound, but the blood pouring from his head somehow left no trace on the ground over which he fled in panic. His screams echoed around the priory as his footsteps receded into the distance.

This haunting took place in Blackfriars Priory, which is situated in Ladybellgate Street in Gloucester and is currently owned by English Heritage. The Dominican priory was built in 1239 where the castle of William the Conqueror once stood. The Scriptorium at the priory is almost certainly the oldest library in England and the friars there were teachers, in addition to being confessors to the rich and powerful. After the Dissolution of the Monasteries in 1539, the priory was bought by Sir Thomas Bell. He split the priory, making one part into a mansion and the other into a factory for the manufacture of knitted hats. This gave a good deal of the population of Gloucester employment and although the hat factory is no longer there, these buildings have been used for industrial purposes ever since.

Various craftsmen such as stonemasons and those employed in the wool trade set up shop at the priory in the eighteenth century and the Great Hall of this building was used as a church and, at a later date, as a school.

The priory is said to be haunted by a number of ghosts, including that of a monk. In 1870 a woman named Alice Godfrey was terrified by the sight of this apparition peering out from under its cowl. She was paralyzed as she stared at the haggard, grey face and wild, staring eyes before her. This sight scared her so much that she promptly fainted.

During restoration work over the last few years, a dungeon has been found and in it the ancient remains of a child. It is said that the fate of this child is in some way connected to the monk who was seen to flee the nave of the church in the priory. In the 1970s, restoration work was being carried out in this nave when the skull of a man with a head wound was found. It is highly likely that it was this man's ghost who was haunting the priory.

In the early 1990s, excavations revealed that the priory cemetery contained many skeletons of women and children. Perhaps this excavation disturbed the ghosts, because in recent times there has been much more spirit activity.

Some who visit the priory say that recently they have heard a child's plaintive cries coming from the location of the dungeon, as well as the monk's heart-stopping screams and his scampering footsteps as he flees in frenzied panic.

# Public House Poltergeists

## GLOUCESTER, GLOUCESTERSHIRE

The much-haunted Dick Whittington public house is located on Westgate Street in Gloucester. This pub's owner tells of many witnesses reporting numerous ghost visitations in recent times and there have also been dozens of accounts of disturbing manifestations in the past.

Westgate Street is an historic thoroughfare that has been travelled by Roman soldiers, English Royalty, Christian martyrs, medieval pilgrims, Civil War soldiers and even Dick Whittington himself. Many people know the tale of a poor boy from Gloucester who went to London with his cat to find his fortune, and his story is retold in the popular pantomime which bears his name.

All these pantomimes follow the same basic plot which describes poor Dick Whittington from Gloucester who, having failed in his quest to make his fortune in the capital city, returns home. Upon reaching Highgate Hill, however, he stops when he hears the bells of London. The bell seems to say to him, 'Turn again Whittington, three times Lord Mayor of London'. He turns back, and eventually overcomes all the obstacles in the way of his success. To crown all his achievements, he is made Lord Mayor of London and subsequently marries his first love, Alice, daughter of Alderman Fitzwarren.

This story it is thought to be based upon the life of a real historical figure, Richard Whittington, the third son of Sir William Whittington, who was born in Pauntley, Gloucestershire, sometime in the late 1350s. Sir William was a reasonably affluent landowner and so his son was not as poor as Dick Whittington is usually portrayed. However, he was still a younger son and in England at that time it was the tradition to practice 'primogeniture', the right of the first born son to inherit the entirety of a parent's wealth. The Normans brought this tradition to England in 1066. Younger sons were left without any inheritance at all, which perhaps prompted Richard Whittington to make his way to London to seek his fortune.

Richard Whittington, it is said, was in some way connected to the spirit world. The bells that rang that day on Highgate Hill were said to have a spectral song accompanying their ringing that only he could hear. Also, he is said to have felt compelled to return to London at that moment, as if a guiding hand were turning him around. Despite his firm commitment to go back to Gloucester, he found himself retracing his steps. Upon his return he apprenticed to the Mercer's company and became prosperous dealing in silks, damasks, velvets and other valuable cloths. He became so successful, in fact, that he gained a very prestigious client indeed – King Richard II. In 1389 Richard Whittington proudly completed his first transaction with the King when he sold his sovereign two pieces of gold cloth for the sum of £11. From then on, the King became a regular customer.

Richard Whittington's dealings with royalty brought him power and political influence and he continued to successfully navigate his business dealings through several successions and the civil instability triggered by these changes. Richard continued on a meteoric rise to success, despite the odds being against him achieving so much so quickly. At the time, it was thought that he had perhaps some otherworldly assistance in his quest for success, although no one went so far as to suggest he had dabbled in the dark arts to gain an advantage.

Richard became well-known, almost famous in fact, through his civic appointments, as during his lifetime he was to become an alderman and sheriff as well as being made Mayor of London. When he died he left his considerable assets to charity. His legacy was also used to found the Greyfriars and Guildhall libraries and to rebuild Newgate Gaol.

Despite many a feline appearance in pantomimes featuring Dick Whittington, it seems that the real Richard Whittington did not, in fact, own a cat. This fantasy was added to the legend more than two centuries after Whittington's death in 1423. The earliest known reference to Dick Whittington's cat can be traced to a comedy about London and its inhabitants called *Eastward Ho!* This production was known to refer to 'the fable of Dick Whittington and his pusse'.

Perhaps Dick Whittington's connection with the spirit world prompted his supposed association with felines. Cats are often thought to have otherworldly connections and have figured prominently in religion and the dark arts throughout antiquity. They were held in high regard by the early Egyptians and were thought to have magical powers. An English twelfth-century religious group called the Cathars worshipped cats and was persecuted by the Church as a result. In some religions, cats represent the form of Satan when they are used in a dark arts ritual mass. Witches were purported to use cats and other small animals to carry out their commands. In this way, a witch would have an alibi when a wicked spell was carried out and be far from the evil act in question.

The first known pantomime using Dick Whittington as the lead character was played in 1814 in Covent Garden. The legend of Dick Whittington and Puss in Boots continues to be embellished and he is still a very popular figure. It is thought that the characters of rats that have been introduced into the pantomimes, for example King Rat, may refer to the Black Death. No doubt these rats were kin to those that inhabited the cellars of the Dick Whittington pub in medieval times and helped to spread the plague. These deaths may have inspired some of the ghosts who still linger in the cellars beneath the building to this day.

Westgate Street threads its way to a bridge over the River Severn which provided the main crossing for trading routes from London and Bristol to South Wales. By the thirteenth century, this street had become the most important market area of Gloucester and various trades established at that time still exist to this day. During medieval times, part of the street was called the Coiffery as numerous hat makers and hairdressers set up business there. Around this time, Westgate Street was divided into two narrow lanes with buildings occupying what is now the middle of the street. These were cleared to make room for the wide street that exists today, but their brick outlines can still be seen.

There is a narrow, spooky tenth-century side street called Mercers Entry which is still in use between the Woolwich and the Stroud & Swindon building societies. Today, Westgate Street is bustling with businesses, shops, restaurants and pubs, many of which spill over into delightful hidden courtyards. The building that houses the Dick Whittington pub at 100 Westgate Street was originally known as Saint Nicholas' House and was used as a family home from the time that it was built in 1311 until 1546.

It is said that a resident ghost regularly haunts the premises. This ghost is described as having a hunched back or as being a hunched figure. He wanders around the bars of the pub and the cellars creating a feeling of foreboding. Customers who experience his apparition are so struck by it that even they cannot blame this sighting on a pint of beer too many. This spectre has been known to jog the elbow of customers with a raised glass, causing them to spill their drink, and has caused such a stir at the pub that the owner has been forced to call in paranormal investigators.

On other numerous occasions white orbs of light have been seen floating in the bar. Sometimes these orbs float around the seat that had always been used by a recently deceased regular customer. Again, this phenomenon cannot be blamed on an excess of alcohol consumed by the witnesses as this scary event has been seen by those who haven't even had their first drink.

Another frequent scary manifestation is that of furniture in the pub moving to different locations – all by itself! This often happens overnight when the pub is locked. There is no explanation for the furniture being completely rearranged behind locked doors with nobody present, unless it is an otherworldly one. Nearly forty years ago, another spectre made his presence known to a crew of workmen who were completing a building project in the cellars of the pub. This spectre was the figure of a man wearing a flat cap. At first the workmen thought this spectre was made of flesh and blood – that is until he walked right through a wall in the cellar. The tough construction types who were working there went weak at the knees, downed tools and fled the pub. Some of them were jabbering with fear as they ran. It is said that all of them refused to continue to work in the cellar – even though it meant that they were subsequently fired.

The Dick Whittington pub must be some kind of haunted hotspot, as there is still more ghost activity in the cellar. When ladies retire to the cloakroom, they have to descend to the seventeenth-century cellar where it is located. These ladies, who are more often than not in a laughing, chatting mood from their revelries in the bar upstairs, are surprised when a sudden change overcomes them. Their light mood disappears because, without fail, as they enter the cloakroom they experience an overwhelming feeling of sadness. This is followed by a terrible attack of fear. The weird, creepy atmosphere that emanates from the cellar is usually so pervasive that several of these customers have fled from the pub after this experience, screaming and in tears.

# Terror at the Tudor House Hotel

## TEWKESBURY, GLOUCESTERSHIRE

The first thing to strike a visitor upon entering the Tudor House Hotel in Tewkesbury is the sight of axe marks on an old oak door leading to a secret garden. This image immediately creates an eerie, spine-chilling atmosphere. The fact that this hotel is home to a number of ghosts is perhaps not surprising, considering its great age and all that has come to pass within its walls.

The Tudor House Hotel was built by the Pilgrim Fathers in 1540 and received a major remodel in 2008. It is now a comfortable, very well-run twenty-two room hostelry which sports the magnificent Adam Suite. This suite, with its four-poster bed and bay window,

*The Tudor House Hotel was built in 1540.*

*Cromwell's soldiers left axe marks here.*

is one of the hotel's salient features. The hotel sits on the High Street in its half-timbered Tudor splendour, ready to take everyone who visits on a trip back in time. The Society for the Preservation of Ancient Buildings has called it one of the best examples in Tewkesbury. It was once the Court of Justice and later the Reverend Samuel Jones ran the Presbyterian Academy within its walls.

It is said that the aforementioned axe marks on the oak door were made by Cromwell and his soldiers, who occupied the hotel during the Civil War in the seventeenth century. In addition to viewing the Tudor House Hotel, visitors can take the Civil War Trail around Tewkesbury which includes a tour of the 'bloody meadow', the site of the battle.

In the Mayor's Parlour, a chimney conceals a priest's hole. After the Dissolution of the Monasteries in 1539, priests were an endangered species and many secreted themselves in hiding places such as this.

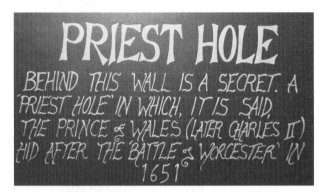

In 1651 the future Charles II hid in the priest's hole by the fireplace.

*A dog's ghost haunts this staircase.*

It seems, however, that it is not a priest that haunts this hotel but the ghost of a woman dressed in a long white gown. This haunting usually begins with her shadowy figure appearing so gradually that an observer is not aware at first that she is an apparition. She is often mistaken for a hotel worker who has entered the room. Startled cries have been heard when the haunted visitor realises that the woman in the long white gown is not actually there. One visitor was known to flee the hotel, leaving everything behind, and had to send for his bag the next day.

A visitor with steadier nerves was haunted by the woman in the white gown and watched her walk through his room. She disappeared, however, before she reached the doorway into the hall. Several other visitors have reported a similar experience. Another ghost that haunts the hotel is that of a black dog. Some say he is a Labrador, but others are not quite sure of his breed. He has been seen several times on the main staircase.

One visitor arrived late on a misty, cold night on his first visit to the hotel and, on his way to his room, saw this same ghost of a dog. He did not believe it was a spectre and walked right up to it as it was in his path. He expected the dog to move aside, but it didn't and he was terrified as he walked right through the apparition.

seven

# CHILLING CHIPPY

Chipping Norton in Oxfordshire and its immediate surroundings seem to be the focus of so much ghost activity that the town and its environs could be likened to an otherworldly Piccadilly Circus during rush hour. There have been so many documented manifestations, in fact, that an entire chapter is needed to describe them.

So tag along, thrill seekers, on a virtual ghost tour of this beautiful area, beginning with Chipping Norton itself, a small, bustling market town south-west of Banbury, and continuing on to other sites within a few miles' radius of the town.

Chipping Norton's chocolate-box-top cottages built of Cotswold limestone turn a delicious golden hue in the setting sun; its Georgian-fronted houses are an architectural delight and its rows of gabled almshouses have become a magnet for photo-snapping tourists. These serene images belie the fact that Chipping Norton, known as 'the Gateway to the Cotswolds', is populated with considerably more ghosts than any other town in this region.

In 1204, the small village of Norton was little more than a few cottages grouped around a church and a castle at the bottom of a hill. But that year, a new market square was laid out on a grand scale with room for vast sheep and cattle pens. Three-day fairs were held and, over time, many craftsmen's houses were built around this square, making the market so important that it became well-known for miles around. Subsequently, the word Chipping was inserted in front of Norton and the town's name was complete. The word 'chipping' is derived from the medieval word for 'market' – chepyne.

Our ghost tour begins from this very same market place, which is still in use today. After that, follow the directions given and refer to the map at the beginning of this chapter.

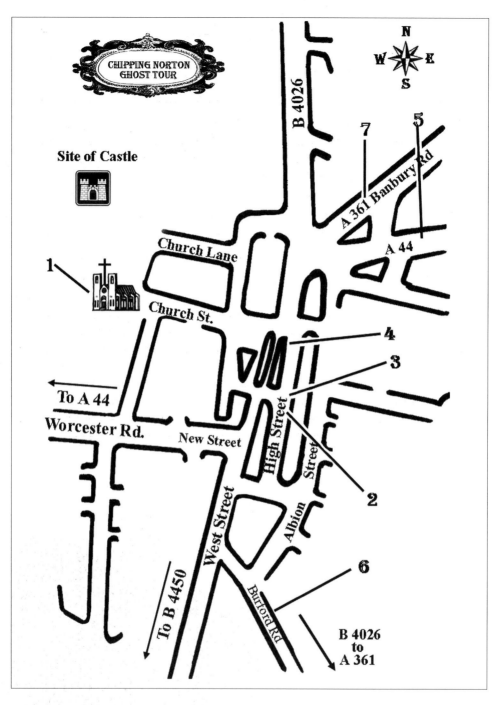

1. *St Mary's Shade – St Mary's Church*
2. *The Crown & Cushion Conspirators –*
   *High Street*
3. *The Stowfair Spook – High Street*

4. *The Haunted White Hart – High Street*
5. *The Creepy Cross Hands – Moreton*
6. *Holt Hotel's Hearthrob – Steeple Aston*
7. *The Rollright Stones Shade's – Long Compton*

# St Mary's Shade

## CHIPPING NORTON, OXFORDSHIRE

*The first stop on the ghost tour is St Mary's Parish Church, which has an impressive nave and some striking brasses. It is an important 'wool' church, built with money earned from the abundant Cotswold sheep. To get to the church, head north along Market Street until you reach Church Street and then turn left (east). A short downhill walk leads to the church.*

*Now, ghost seekers, hold on to your hats and perhaps be prepared for a few more spine-tingling, hair-raising chills than had been anticipated.*

It is well documented that the largely perpendicular St Mary's Parish Church in Chipping Norton is haunted, and certainly any visitor who casts a glance at the ceiling of the south hexagonal porch would understand why a ghost might feel quite at home there. Staring back at the visitor are the faces of grotesque devils and Green Men, their expressions twisted into horrible grimaces. These amazingly ugly faces, carved hundreds of years ago, are sculpted onto bosses that are attached to the centre of each section of the vaulted porch ceiling.

During medieval times this porch was a busy part of the church where civil business and religious rites were conducted. Stone benches were placed around the perimeter of the porch to accommodate the townspeople who came for baptismal services, marriage banns, absolution for penitents, to collect legacies or to gather for Church processions.

*St Mary's Church is haunted by a hanged vicar.*

There is evidence of a church dating from the twelfth century on this site, but a new church appears to have been built over the original and then enlarged in the fourteenth century. There were no other renovations to the church until 1893 when the tower became unstable and was pulled down and reconstructed. A local priest was said to have been hanged from the earlier tower and his ghost haunts Chipping Norton to this day.

This came about following the Reformation. At this time the financial distress caused by the enclosure of lands and economic inflation put a huge monetary strain on the parish. In addition, the church was ordered to use Cranmer's *Book of Common Prayer* in English. This was very unpopular with the laity. They preferred the familiar Latin but all Latin books had been destroyed on orders from the Crown. The burden of the purchase of all new prayer books led to a revolt by the vicar, Henry Joyce, and his three neighbouring incumbents. This revolt was quickly put down by the local squires and Henry Joyce, who had begun his tenure as vicar in 1546, was hanged from the tower of St Mary's Church in 1549.

To this day this poor cleric's apparition walks forlornly about the town, exactly as if he were still alive. There have been many sightings of his shade.

# The Crown & Cushion Conspirators

## CHIPPING NORTON, OXFORDSHIRE

*The next stop is the Crown & Cushion Hotel. Return along Church Street and continue walking, crossing West Street on the way until the High Street is reached. Next, turn right (south) and cross the street. Continue walking a few steps to 23 High Street, which is the Crown & Cushion inn.*

A crowd of ghosts haunt the old Crown & Cushion Hotel on Chipping Norton High Street. This fifteenth-century coaching inn, now a comfortable, well-run hotel, was once the meeting place of a gang of conspirators who hatched the Gunpowder Plot in 1605. The uncovering of this plot is still commemorated by Guy Fawkes Night celebrations every year on 5 November. These conspirators are said to have haunted the bar of this hotel since this time and have scared many inhabitants of the town over the centuries.

One of the leaders of this plot was Robert Catesby, who was once the owner of nearby Chastleton House. Catesby sold this house to Walter Jones, who then tore it down and rebuilt it, and Chastleton House has remained completely unchanged since this rebuilding was completed in 1612. This house was handed over to the National Trust in 1991 after 400 years of continuous ownership by the same family, and its contents and features have been in use for this entire time. Because the National Trust adopted a groundbreaking policy of restoring Chastleton House 'as is', with its soot-covered walls in the kitchen and its abandoned slipper bath in the roof, a visit to this house is like a journey back in time. The house's medieval furniture and disintegrating wall hangings

*The Crown & Cushion Inn in earlier times.*

*Ghosts of the plotters meet here.*

*A ghostly Gunpowder Plot conspirator is associated with Chastleton House.*

are in stark contrast to modern-day comforts and produce a cold, ghostly atmosphere. As Catesby seems to have become one of the undead after his involvement in the Gunpowder Plot, it seems a fitting that he once owned a house on this site. Chastleton House is now administered by the National Trust and can be viewed by appointment.

Catesby, an ardent Catholic, decided to take action after less and less tolerance was shown to those of his religion under the rule of King James I. His plan was to blow up the King and the Houses of Parliament, thereby inciting a rebellion that would gain him enough support to install a Catholic head of state. The explosives needed for this plot were to be supplied by his co-conspirator Guy Fawkes, whose military training had made him an expert in this field.

Catesby and his gang's plot to kill King James I involved tunnelling under the House of Lords from a house leased nearby. The gunpowder they were to use would be laid and detonated from there. Catesby owned another house in Lambeth and used it to store the thirty-six barrels of explosives and the necessary mining equipment for a tunnel. But this plot began to unravel from the outset as a Parliamentary meeting in the House of Lords, which would have brought all of Catesby's enemies together, was postponed due to illness and death brought on by the plague.

Also, so much time elapsed after the explosives were hidden beneath winter fuel in a coal cellar under the House of Lords that details of the plot leaked out. This was certainly fortunate for many of the politicians and citizens of London, for in the event that all the barrels of gunpowder had exploded, a huge area of the city would have been decimated. This would have included the Old Palace of Westminster, Westminster Abbey and all the adjoining buildings.

*Ghosts often mingle with guests at the bar.*

Details given by an informant led to a search of the cellars below the House of Lords and, at midnight on 5 November, Guy Fawkes was discovered hiding near the barrels of gunpowder and in possession of ignition paper and matches. He admitted his intentions and was then tortured until he named his accomplices. Catesby had already fled but was subsequently caught and killed in a gun battle. Some of the other conspirators were captured and horribly tortured before being put on trial. The public were jubilant when they heard that the Gunpowder Plot had been foiled and, as a result, the trial was mobbed.

Four of the conspirators were executed in St Paul's churchyard and the remainder were hanged, drawn and quartered. Guy Fawkes managed to avoid a slow death by jumping from the gallows with a noose around his neck. He died instantly, but when his co-conspirator Robert Keyes tried the same manoeuvre, his rope severed and he was disembowelled while fully conscious.

Over the years, many visitors to the Crown & Cushion Hotel have had their enjoyment of a quiet pint of beer disturbed by the sudden appearance of the ghosts of Robert Catesby and his gang crowding together in the corner of the bar as they whisper the secrets of their deadly Gunpowder Plot.

# The Stowfair Spook

## CHIPPING NORTON, OXFORDSHIRE

*Now, a stroll along Chipping Norton High Street is suggested before returning to the market place. The spook described below is often encountered in this area at night... but has sometimes been seen in the daylight hours too.*

This mercurial manifestation, known as the Stowfair Man, haunts the town mostly after dark and only during the months of May and October. His form is indistinct and shadowy and, at times, he is half-transparent. No one knows how he came by his name, but he seems to be familiar to many of the local townspeople who have seen him wandering around the High Street and the churchyard. His regular-as-clockwork appearances for the entire month of May and then again in October have become almost humdrum to the townspeople.

As he walks around the town he picks up ordinary objects and makes them disappear. A few seconds later he will replace these objects, making them instantly reappear. He seems quite proud of this trick and scares the life out of people hurrying past who may have thought that his shadowy figure was real. Many unwary visitors have been reduced to pale, stuttering, wild-eyed blobs after having just seen the Stowfair Man place his hand on a street bench and – poof, its gone! Just as suddenly, when the Stowfair Man moves away, this same bench reappears.

# The Haunted White Hart

## CHIPPING NORTON, OXFORDSHIRE

*The next stop on the ghost tour will be on the north side of the market square, where a newly-remodelled, elegant block of flats now occupies the site that was previously the White Hart. The original coach entrance into a courtyard is still standing and, in addition, this tasteful conversion still retains many of the original features of the centuries-old inn. Some say it also retains its centuries-old ghosts.*

Archaeologists have reported evidence of a building on the site of this old coaching inn from as early as the twelfth century. Whatever was erected then has been rebuilt numerous times over the years and before the inn was converted, there was a gallery that extended from one side of the yard to the other. The remainder of the inn seems to have been almost completely remodelled in the eighteenth century. Next, the façade was rebuilt in the 1930s in order to restore it to its eighteenth-century character.

*The entrance of the White Hart Hotel.*

There have been a number of sightings of ghosts who reputedly haunted the bedrooms of the White Hart over the centuries. A seventeenth-century inventory that was found of the inn described, together with other details, the names of the bedrooms during those times; the Worcester Chamber, the Hereford Chamber, the Queen's Arms Chamber, the Great Chamber and the Gatehouse Chamber were among the names used.

Another chamber known as the Oak Room was said to be haunted by a number of ghosts. A magnificent, four-poster oak bed was this suite's main feature and, apparently, one ghost was seen opening a secret door that was hidden in the oak-panelled walls, slipping into the room and scaring the wits out of its occupant.

Some time in the future, no doubt, there will be yet another chapter to write about the ghosts who haunt this building from the occupants of the new conversion.

# The Creepy Cross Hands

## MORETON, OXFORDSHIRE

*This stop requires a car ride to nearby Salford Hill on the A44 road, opposite the junction with the A436 Stow road between Chipping Norton and Moreton. The destination is Moreton's Pub and Restaurant, which was formerly the Cross Hands Inn.*

The haunted Cross Hands Inn, a 600-year-old pub, has recently been renamed Moreton's Pub and Restaurant. New management notwithstanding, however, the extremely old ghosts that haunt the inn have decided to stay on and continue to make it their home. There have been a number of spooky manifestations at the inn throughout the years, occurring at regularly spaced intervals.

Previous owners of the inn once saw a woman in an old-fashioned dress walk across the bar and then suddenly disappear into thin air. On another occasion the owners detected a strong smell of perfume as they descended the stairs and, at another time, a woman's voice was heard calling throughout the inn. This happened late at night and was heard particularly loudly in a low-beamed hallway when the inn was known to be empty. A thorough search of the inn revealed nobody. This same 'calling woman' was also heard by the owner's son. On yet another very scary occasion, when the owners knew the inn to be empty, a door was kicked in with great violence.

All these visitations happened intermittently over the years until a recent car crash damaged the building. This seemed to infuriate these ghosts and caused them to stage a mass haunting. These apparitions called in reinforcements to join them in making their protests loud and clear, and let everybody on the other side know that they were angrier than a stirred-up nest of hornets. The hauntings were suddenly so frequent that the restaurant's staff were seriously disturbed.

The car crash that caused this massive manifestation punched a 12ft by 12ft hole through a wall in this lovely old pub, trapping the driver for about an hour before he could be extricated and taken to hospital, where he was treated for non-life threatening injuries. The ghosts had such a tantrum about being disturbed that a team from the Ghostfinder Paranormal Society was called in to investigate. The society found it necessary to bring along high-tech equipment to document changes in the electromagnetic field.

The foot-stomping spooks put on quite a show, apparently confirming the notion that ghosts often step up their activities when repair or remodelling work is done on old buildings. Sudden temperature drops from toasty to below freezing were an hourly occurrence. These manifestations were very eerie. A typical example involved an employee standing in front of a warm fire who suddenly felt colder than if he were wading in an icy river.

Various other incidents have occurred, including: the ghost of a woman who paraded up and down the corridors and entered bedrooms, scaring the occupants into fleeing the hotel; a CD player was found blasting out music when employees entered the inn in the morning, even though it had been switched off the night before; floating orbs whizzed around the rooms at all hours of the day and night, and wailing was sometimes heard early in the morning. It seems that these hauntings will continue until the inn is repaired and, in the meantime, anyone who visits the building experiences chills like they have never known before.

# Holt Hotel's Heartthrob

## STEEPLE ASTON, OXFORDSHIRE

*Next is the Holt Hotel, a few miles south-east of Chipping Norton and close to the junction of the B4030 and A4260 Banbury road. There is a great deal of otherworldly unrest at this fifteenth-century coaching inn, for it has a very gory history of murders and mayhem.*

This inn is famous for being haunted by a French highwayman named Claude Du Vall. He apparently fancied himself as some kind of medieval Don Juan, making conquests of women wherever he went. He was such a ladies man, in fact, that he was said to romance his female victims even as he was robbing them.

This 'love 'em, loot 'em and leave 'em' highwayman known as 'Dashing Du Vall' was born in Normandy and made his way to England as the valet of the Duke of Richmond. He must have envied his affluent master's lifestyle because he set about creating a similar one of his own. He assembled a gang and took to a life of crime, holding up stagecoaches on lonely country roads.

Whenever Monsieur Du Vall attacked a stagecoach, the women on board would be appraised and flirted with even before any valuables were taken. On one occasion, after Du Vall had held up a stagecoach, he was so entranced with the wife of one of his victims that he insisted on dancing with her right there on the road as his gang continued to train their pistols on the remaining occupants of the coach. When this brief minuet was over, Du Vall robbed the lady's husband of £100.

It seems that despite the fact that he was a murdering thief, Du Vall had excellent manners. This fact was proved when, on one occasion, a member of his gang seized the silver feeding bottle of a stagecoach victim who was the mother of a young baby. Apparently, Du Vall returned the feeding bottle when the baby cried.

After a hold up that produced a particularly good haul, Du Vall and his gang celebrated at the Holt Hotel. During this bacchanalian jaunt, Du Vall lost no time in romancing the innkeeper's daughter. The festivities went on far into the night, however, and loose talk among the drunken gang members led to the innkeeper discovering that his guests, who were merrily drinking and debauching under his very roof, were, in fact, a murderous highway gang. He immediately informed the authorities and Du Vall and his associates were arrested and taken to London.

Shortly thereafter, Du Vall was sentenced to be executed at Tyburn. The following speaks of Duvall's 'bags of charm' because, upon his sentencing, many of his female victims relentlessly petitioned for his pardon. A good number of these women came from the highest families in the land, but even their rank could not sway the authorities and the sentence was carried out. Du Vall was hanged in 1670 and buried in Covent Garden. His grave is now long gone, but at the time his headstone had the following epitaph carved upon it:

Here lies Duvall, if male thou art, look to your purse, if female to thy heart.

Immediately following Du Vall's execution, a grisly discovery was made at the Holt Hotel. The innkeeper who had turned Du Vall over to the authorities, together with his family, were found bludgeoned to death in their beds. Although the perpetrators of this crime were never called to justice, it was thought by many that the evil ghosts of Du Vall and his gang were responsible for this horrible crime.

Du Vall haunts the Holt Hotel to this day and has been seen on many occasions floating around the guest rooms and the bar. When this happens, drinking glasses whiz off shelves, creepy, choking sounds can be heard simultaneously in several rooms and icy-cold areas are experienced by hotel guests. This ghoulish, romancing robber also likes to make frequent appearances in bedroom No. 3 of the hotel.

It seems that there have been many other incidents during this ancient building's history that have initiated still more hauntings, given that several other ghosts have joined Du Vall in visitations at the Holt Hotel. As a result, it has become a popular spot for those who court the company of the paranormal. Group séances with psychics, tours of the most actively haunted locations and Ouija board sessions are all held regularly at the hotel and many sightings of Claude Du Vall and his cohorts have been reported. So ladies beware! If you are staying at the Holt Hotel and a particularly handsome, charismatic man wearing old-fashioned clothes and speaking with a smooth-as-silk French accent tries to romance you, pinch him to see if he is real before you fall instantly in love and surrender to his suave charms.

# The Rollright Stones' Shades

## LONG COMPTON, OXFORDSHIRE

> *Now for the final site – the Rollright Stones. These straddle the Oxfordshire / Warwickshire border, a few miles north-east of Chipping Norton off the A3400 road near the village of Long Compton.*

The Rollright Stones are a collection of huge, haunted monuments somewhat similar in appearance to Stonehenge. They are thought to be from the Neolithic or Bronze Age and are arranged in three separate sites. One set of stones is called the Whispering Knights

*One of the King's Men.*

and is said to be haunted by all manner of witches, ghosts and other evil manifestations. Located nearby is the King Stone, and the third grouping is known as the King's Men.

A folktale handed down through the centuries tells of an ancient King and his army who were riding across the county when they reached this area and were hailed by a witch. The King, curious to hear what she had to say, halted with his men. The witch cackled as she intoned the following sentence: 'Seven long strides thou shalt take, and if Long Compton thou canst see, King of England thou shalt be!'

The King took up the witch's challenge and took seven long strides towards Long Compton. But as the King moved towards this village, which was located in a valley off in the distance, a hill blocked his vision and he could not see it. When this happened, the witch's evil and sinister laugh echoed through the valley and she proclaimed the following words: 'As Long Compton thou canst not see, King of England thou shalt not be! Rise up stick and stand still stone, for King of England thou shalt be none. Thou and thy men hoar stones shall be, and I myself an elder tree!'

The King instantly turned into what is now known as the King Stone, which stands alone. Today, this is a somewhat broken-down monolith, 8ft high by 5ft wide, and stands approximately 250ft east of the next grouping of stones known as the King's Men. Members of the King's army had been standing in a circle around the King when the witch is supposed to have turned them into the circle of stones as well, forming this second grouping.

Today, the King's Men grouping consists of seventy closely spaced stones forming a circle 108ft in diameter. These stones are set on top of a circular bank. Two portal stones mark the entrance to this bank, which is to the south-east of the King Stone. This site was restored in 1882. It is considered unlucky to touch the King's Men stones. To do so is thought to disturb their ghosts. Should this happen, there is the possibility that these ghosts will haunt the person who has touched the stone for the remainder of their lives.

Next, the witch prepared to turn herself into an elder tree but, at this point, she noticed four of the King's knights who had lagged behind and were now making a late arrival. With a great cackle of glee, the witch also then turned these four knights into stone. Some say these men were lagging behind because they were traitors who were cooking up a conspiracy to overthrow the King. They are known as the third grouping – the Whispering Knights.

The Whispering Knights appear to be what is left of an early or middle Neolithic portal dolmen that had been the entrance to a burial chamber. Four stones survive and are situated 1,312ft east of the King's Men grouping. These four stones form a chamber about 6.5ft square and surround a fifth stone, now toppled over, which was most likely a roof capstone.

Folklore passed down from the eighteenth century tells of the local custom of a meeting of village maids who would gather on Midsummer's Eve to listen for voices emanating from the Whispering Knights' stones. It is said that they would hear about their future fate from the soft winds wafting around these stones. If they were lucky and listened extremely closely, these gentle zephyrs would turn into human voices and foretell the events of their lives.

There are many other strange manifestations and ghost activities around the Rollright Stones, which is a place full of foreboding either at midday or midnight. The strange, erratic shapes of the stones viewed in an early morning fog or in the mist during a full moon on a windy night seem to take on human form and have been known to terrify any pets who accompany observers to the stones. In addition, local farmers tell of livestock that has been lost from fields near the Rollright Stones. The farm gates to these fields are mysteriously found open by morning, even though they have been fastened with padlocks the night before.

The Rollright Stones are centered upon an important cluster of ley lines. Studies of ley lines, earth energy and other such manifestations report that the lines lead through Wroxton and Copredy to Arbury Camp. Also significant are energy lines that are said to connect the stones and lead on into the countryside. This information was reported in the book *Ley Hunter's Companion* by Devereux and Thomson.

In *The Ghosts and Witches of the Cotswolds* by J.A. Brooks, the author tells of a farmer from one of the nearby villages who relayed his attempt to move a Rollright Stone that had toppled to the ground many centuries before. He used a team of strong horses to accomplish this task. He wished to cover a culvert near his cottage, thinking the stone would serve well as a bridge. Even though the team of horses he used was considered strong enough for this task, the stone had only been dragged a few yards when the horses became strangely terrified. These animals reared and bucked, making horrific whinnying sounds and were finally unable to continue. The farmer realised that some strange haunting was causing this effect and decided to return the stone to its original position a few days later. He was able to do so using only a single horse with no problem whatsoever.

Legend has it, too, that at midnight on certain nights of the year the stones come alive and anybody present at that time is haunted by the ghosts of the King and his men. When the moon is high, these men appear to return to flesh and bone and are seen, in their ancient battle dress, dancing and jousting around the stones as if the victory of a great battle is being celebrated and all is well. Supposedly anyone who looks upon these festive antics either turns to stone or dies on the spot.

The Chipping Norton ghost tour ends here and all the ghost hunters who have, with a little luck, encountered a ghoul or two should by now be shivering and shaking with fear – which is just the way a thrill-seeking spirit watcher should finish up.

# SOURCES

*Books*

Betjeman, John, *Trains and Buttered Toast* (John Murray, 2006)
Brooks, J.A., *The Ghosts and Witches of the Cotswolds* (Jarrold Publishing, 1997)
Harding, Mike, *A Little Book of Gargoyles* (Arum Press, 1998)
Titchmarsh, Peter, *The Cotswolds Town and Village Guide* (Reardon Publishing, 2000)


*Guidebooks*

Chavenage House guidebook
Kelmscott Manor guidebook
National Trust guidebooks


*Websites*

www.aboutbritain.com
www.allsands.com/History/People/spirits
   legends_ia_gn.htm
www.banbury-cross.co.uk
www.bbc.co.uk/legacies
www.beehive.thisisbath.com
www.britainexpress.com
www.costwolds.com
www.focusonfaringdon.co.uk
www.ghosts-uk.net
www.ghost-story.co.uk
www.gloucestercivictrust.org.uk
www.hauntedhotelguide.com
www.faringdon.org/hysoc.htm
www.livinggloucester.co.uk
www.longislandgothic.com
www.mystical.co.uk
www.nationaltrust.org.uk

www.owlpen.com
www.paranormaldatabase.com
www.paranormalnights.co.uk
www.paranormalresearchgroup.com
www.picturesofengland.com
www.soglos.com
www.spiritforum.com
www.telegraph.co.uk
www.topparanormalsites.com
www.travelaroundeurope.co.uk
www.unexplainable.net
www.wikipedia.com
www.wospweb.com

# Other titles published by The History Press

## Haunted Worcestershire
ANTHONY POULTON-SMITH

Contained within the pages of this book are strange tales of spectral sightings, active poltergeists and restless spirits appearing in streets, inns, churches, estates, public buildings and private homes across the area. This new collection of stories, a product of both historical accounts and numerous interviews conducted with local witnesses, is sure to appeal to all those intrigued by Worcestershire's haunted heritage.

978 0 7524 4872 5

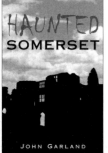

## Haunted Somerset
JOHN GARLAND

Drawing on historical and contemporary sources, *Haunted Somerset* reveals its uniquely supernatural heritage, including a coffin on the road, eerie Bath, the phantoms of Sedgemoor, Dunster Castle's ghostly sightings, headless horsemen, animal apparitions and Exmoor spectres – and if these are not enough to curdle your nervous system, a screaming skull and the grisly haunting associated with a curate murdered by some of his parishioners who was rumoured to have been cannibalised!

978 0 7524 4335 5

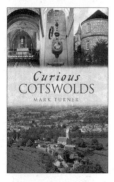

## Curious Cotswolds
MARK TURNER

*Curious Cotswolds* takes the reader on a tour of the area, looking at the history, archaeology and curiosities of the Cotswolds. The author, a former Cotswolds policeman, describes points of interest to be found in the towns, villages and hamlets of the region, looking at Cheltenham and North; Cirencester, Stroud and South; Worcestershire and Warwickshire; and Oxfordshire.

978 0 7524 3930 3

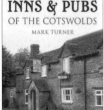

## Inns & Pubs of the Cotswolds
MARK TURNER

This A-Z covering Gloucestershire, Oxfordshire, Warwickshire and Worcestershire is a delightful tour around the most interesting pubs in the area. Taking in all manner of establishments, such as the Coach and Horses, an old village pub in Longborough, to the White Hart Royal Hotel, a sixteenth-century inn in Moreton-on-Marsh, the author visits a huge variety of pubs that have made the Cotswolds the charmingx area it is today.

978 0 7524 4465 9

Visit our website and discover thousands of other History Press books.
**www.thehistorypress.co.uk**